# Flint Flushwork

## A MEDIEVAL MASONRY ART

## Stephen Hart

With Photographs by the Author

The Boydell Press

Flint Flushwork: A Medieval Masonry Art

© Stephen Hart 2008

All Rights Reserved. Except as permitted under current legislation no part of this work may be photocopied, stored in a retrieval system, published, performed in public, adapted, broadcast, transmitted, recorded or reproduced in any form or by any means, without the prior permission of the copyright owner.

The views expressed in this volume reflect the views of the authors, and not necessarily those of the editors or publisher.

First published 2008
The Boydell Press, Woodbridge

ISBN 978-1-84383-369-7

The Boydell Press is an imprint of Boydell & Brewer Ltd
Whitwell House, St Audry's Park Road, Melton, Woodbridge, Suffolk, IP12 1SY, UK
and of Boydell & Brewer Inc.
668 Mt Hope Avenue, Rochester, NY 14620, USA
website: www.boydellandbrewer.com

A CIP catalogue record for this book is available from the British Library

Front cover images:
    top – Woolpit church, Suffolk.
    bottom – Cromer, Norfolk.

Unless otherwise stated all images are copyright of the author.

Printed and bound in Great Britain by
CPI Antony Rowe, Chippenham, Wiltshire

# *Contents*

| | |
|---|---|
| Introduction | vii |
| Chapter 1 What is Flushwork? | 1 |
| Chapter 2 Flushwork Themes | 9 |
|     Inset Flushwork | 9 |
|     Imitation Windows | 10 |
|     Chequer Flushwork | 11 |
|     Flushwork Emblems | 14 |
|     Flushwork Panelling | 17 |
|     Inscriptions | 21 |
|     Wavy Flushwork | 22 |
| Chapter 3 Themes with Affinity to Flushwork | 23 |
|     Brick Flushwork | 23 |
|     Flushwork with Unknapped Flints | 24 |
|     Carstone Flushwork | 26 |
|     Proudwork | 26 |
| Chapter 4 The Architectural Setting | 29 |
|     Tower Parapets | 29 |
|     Church Towers | 33 |
|     Porches | 35 |
|     Clerestories | 38 |
|     Chancels, Chapels and Aisles | 40 |
|     Buttresses | 42 |
|     Secular Buildings | 44 |
| Chapter 5 Kindred Features | 65 |
| The Gazetteer | 71 |
|     Norfolk | 72 |
|     Suffolk | 111 |
|     Essex | 157 |
|     Cambridgeshire | 165 |
|     Bedfordshire | 167 |
|     Buckinghamshire | 167 |
|     Hertfordshire | 167 |
|     Surrey | 168 |
| Appendix A. Buildings with Proudwork | 169 |
| Appendix B. Churches with Brick Flushwork | 171 |
| Appendix C. Shallow-sunk Stone Heads to Flushwork Panels | 172 |
| Appendix D. 'Norwich' Style Flushwork on Church Tower Parapets | 173 |
| Bibliography | 175 |

# List of Illustrations

1. Rubble flint.
2. Knapped flint.
3. West Somerton church. Belfry.
4. Theberton church. Belfry.
5. Elmswell church. South aisle.

Fig 1 Abstract flushwork design.

6. Griston church. Tower parapet.
7. Hanging Langford, Wilts. Lapped chequer.
8. Southolt church porch.
9. Elmswell church. Mouchettes.
10. Woodbridge church. Marian monogram.
11. Grundisburgh church. Lily in vase.
12. Great Cressingham church. Crowned sword.
13. Elmswell church. Catherine wheel.
14. Northwold church. Pommée cross.
15. Hawstead church. Three emblems.
16. Finningham church porch. Shallow stone sinkings.
17. Trefoiled panels.
18. Cinquefoiled panels.
19. Canopied panels.
20. Supermullioned panels.
21. Tiered panels, straight-headed.
22. Tiered panels, castellated heads.
23. Tiered panels, Canopy-headed.
24. Halesworth church porch. Paired panels.
25. Paired panels with shared crocketted canopy head.
26. Swannington church porch. Lombardic script inscription.
27. Stratford St Mary church. Gothic script inscription.
28. Ufford church porch. Wavy ornament.
29. Norwich, St Benedict's church tower. Brick flushwork.
30. Dickleburgh church tower parapet. Unknapped flint panel infilling.
31. Burnham Norton Friary Gatehouse. Proudwork.
32. North Tuddenham church tower parapet. Proudwork.
33. Brome church porch. Shallow-recessed flint panel infilling.

Fig 2 Typical tower parapet formats.

34. Althorne church tower parapet. Lattice flushwork.
35. Redenhall church tower. East wall.
36. Worstead church tower. Flushwork dado.
37. Beachamwell church tower. Belfry.
38. Hitcham church porch.
39. Wortham church clerestory.
40. Earl Stonham church clerestory.
41. Rattlesden church clerestory.
42. Mutford church. Flushwork dado on chancel east wall.
43. Norwich, St Michael at Coslany. South aisle.
44. Dalham church tower.
45. Pulham St Mary church porch buttress.
46, 47, 48, 49 St Ethelbert's Gate, Norwich.
50. St Osyth's Priory Gatehouse.
51. Coltishall church tower, west wall.
52. Thrandeston church tower base.

Fig 3 Map of East Anglia.

53. Beeston St Lawrence church. Flushwork dado on chancel east wall.
54. Breckles church tower. Belfry.
55. Deopham church tower parapet.
56. Great Massingham church tower buttress.
57. Martham church. Chancel buttress.
58. Norwich, St Clement's church tower parapet.
59. Poringland church tower. Belfry.
60. Potter Heigham church tower. Belfry.
61. Thompson church. Tower base.
62. Wymondham Abbey clerestory.
63. Bungay, St Mary's church. Tower west window arch.
64. Coddenham church. South aisle parapet.
65. Creeting St Mary church porch.
66. Earl Stonham church tower parapet.
67. Gipping church. Nave window.
68. Halesworth church tower parapet.
69. Horham church tower base.
70. Kedington church tower.
71. Kersey church porch.
72. Little Waldingfield church tower parapet.
73. Long Melford church. Lady Chapel.
74. Market Weston church porch.
75. Metfield porch, buttress detail.
76. Southwold church tower west wall.
77. Walsham le Willows church porch.
78. Worlingworth church porch.
79. Ardleigh church tower parapet.
80. Brightlingsea, flushwork panel detail.
81. Great Bromley church porch.
82. Lawford church tower.
83. Bottisham church. South aisle.

# List of Colour Plates

| | | |
|---|---|---|
| Frontispiece | Barsham church. Chancel east wall. | |
| I | Southwold church porch. | 49 |
| II | Great Witchingham church. | 50 |
| III | Little Walsingham Priory ruins. | 51 |
| IV | Hopton church. | 52 |
| V | East Tuddenham church porch. | 53 |
| VI | Ixworth Thorpe church porch. | 54 |
| VII | Papworth St Agnes church. | 55 |
| VIII | Salcott church porch. | 56 |
| IX | Kersey church tower parapet. | 57 |
| X | Lawford church. Chancel wall. | 57 |
| XI | Redenhall church tower. | 58 |
| XII | Ipswich, St Lawrence's church tower. | 59 |
| XIII | Woolpit church clerestory. | 60 |
| XIV | Cavendish church clerestory. | 60 |
| XV | Chelmsford Cathedral porch. | 61 |
| XVI | Great Barton church. | 62 |
| XVII | Castle Acre Priory, Prior's Lodging outer porch. | 63 |
| XVIII | Barton Bendish, St Andrew's church porch. | 64 |

Frontispiece: Barsham Church. Lattice pattern of the flushwork on the chancel east wall extended across the window as mullions. This extraordinary example was probably produced in the sixteenth century.

# Introduction

Flushwork is a wholly external decorative medium, and so, despite many churches having to be kept locked as a precaution against theft and vandalism, it is an artistic achievement that can be viewed whether or not a church is open, and with a large number displaying some form of flushwork, there is a rich field of study. Surprisingly however, it has not in the past attracted the same depth of research and analysis as other aspects of church architecture.

Conceived as a companion work to the author's *Flint Architecture of East Anglia*, in which classifications were devised for the many ways that flint has been used in the walls of buildings, this book provides a wider perspective of the several different modes of Flushwork that were identified in that book. By elucidating the various strands of this relatively uncharted branch of church art and showing how they have been used on buildings, the book aims to foster a wider understanding and enjoyment of its imagery and spectacle, and through greater acceptance of its historical importance as a medieval decorative technique, to encourage sympathetic restoration of those many flushwork motifs and inscriptions that have lost their flint infillings. It may perhaps also stimulate a revival of the craft through a recognition by today's architects that innovative interpretation of flushwork to create modern works of art could re-establish it as a decorative medium appropriate to contemporary buldings in flint regions.

Symbolic emblems and inscriptions constitute a characteristic part of the flushwork tradition, and although this book includes descriptions of some of the motifs commonly used, it does not seek to provide detailed interpretations of them at individual churches as this has been well done elsewhere recently – notably in the scholarly *Decoding Flint Flushwork on Suffolk and Norfolk Churches* by John Blatchly and Peter Northeast.

Acknowledgements are due to Norfolk County Council Library and Information Service for permission to reproduce illustrations nos. 46 and 48: these are taken from Britton's *History and Antiquities of the See and Cathedral Church of Norwich*, 1815.

In the text and gazetteer, figures in parentheses are the reference numbers of the illustrations, those in Roman numerals refer to the coloured ones.

CHAPTER ONE

# What is Flushwork?

In much of England's chalkland, which includes about half of East Anglia, the land, cliffs and beaches abound with an unlimited harvest of flint. Originating in the chalk, flint nodules encrusted with a white rind known as the cortex, have over millions of years been eroded from their parent rock and, often modified by various geological processes, deposited on coastlines and in inland beds as gravels and shingles or in the soil as fragmented nodules and cobbly boulders.

Extracted from chalk and gravel pits or gathered from the fields and beaches, these indigenous flints have since Saxon times been the chief walling materials of most East Anglian churches, particularly in Norfolk and Suffolk, although for some time, they were used only in their natural 'as-found' state and laid as rubble (plate 1), randomly or in courses.

plate 1. Rubble flint.

plate 2. Knapped flint.

Many centuries earlier, however, as can be seen in the mighty walls of Burgh Castle at the mouth of the River Waveney, the Romans had known how to split flints to give them a flat surface and to trim them to regular shapes, but thereafter the knack seems to have been lost for a thousand years. These skills, called knapping, were not rediscovered until the late thirteenth century when the earliest medieval walls faced entirely with deliberately split flints appear. Thereafter, the use of knapped flint (plate 2) for facing work increased, particularly for high quality buildings, as for example in the mid-fourteenth-century enlargements of the Prior's quarters at Castle Acre Priory. They were also often combined with as-found flints and with other small stones from distant sources deposited locally in glacial subsoils as erratics.

The cut face of a flint looks quite different from its crusty cortex and has a silky texture with an almost vitreous lustre and initially is usually black; once exposed though, the darkness of the core seemingly starts imperceptibly to pale, producing in due course, perhaps over hundreds of years, shades of blue-black fading to blue-grey as ageing progresses. Today, we can see subtle hues ranging from dark to light in the knapped flints of medieval buildings which may well have been uniformly black when laid. But not all flint cores were black; plain or mottled shades of brown, olive, amber and grey are also found though less commonly, and in one area in North-East Norfolk several churches can show knapped flintwork of almost pure white.

Flint has been widely used for building in most of the chalkland districts of England, and walls of knapped flint and stone laid in chequer patterns or bands were not unusual in flint areas where stone was also available locally, like in parts of Wiltshire and Dorset. East Anglia has no comparable freestones but after the Norman Conquest, limestones from quarries on the Lincolnshire Limestone formation were imported into the region, and in the early fourteenth century their imaginative use as ashlar in combination with indigenous knapped flints heralded the emergence of a vibrant style of architectural decoration, transcending the simple geometry of chequers and banding. Comparable in masonry to inlaid work in furniture, and exploiting the contrast between the mellow shades and textures of limestone ashlar and the lustre of fractured flint, these two materials were set flush with each other in compositions to form architectural patterns and decorative or symbolic motifs on the external walls of flint buildings. This innovative art-form, now known as flushwork, is found mainly on churches although there are a few examples on secular buildings. It was a phenomenon that flourished memorably in East Anglia wherein stand more than five hundred churches with flushwork decoration on some part of their structure; over ninety per cent of them lie to the east of a dog-leg line Cromer–Newmarket–Colchester, the others being more widely spread beyond those bounds, one of them, surprisingly in the Cambridgeshire fens at March, some distance from flint country.

The stone elements of flushwork patterns are almost invariably formed with limestone ashlar but there are rare exceptions; unique, perhaps, is the much-repaired fourteenth-century tower of Lawford church where in the remnants of a flushwork composition, a surviving knapped flint panel is framed by strips of dark brown 'puddingstone', probably a local iron-indurated gravel stone (plate 82). Elsewhere, in the Foulness peninsular, one or two churches have rough ragstone in the squares of their chequerwork.

Although it cannot be dated more closely than perhaps the late thirteenth or early fourteenth century, the first use of knapped flint in association with ashlar stone to form architectural decoration may have been in the replica windows in alternate facets of the octagonal belfry of the cobble-flint round tower of West Somerton church (plate 3). These blank windows copy the lancet form of the belfry openings in the cardinal faces of the octagon and have ashlar stone dressings to their jambs and arches, but the 'openings' are infilled with squared knapped flints set flush with the outer surface of the surrounding stone

plate 3. Blank replica windows infilled with knapped flint in the belfry of West Somerton church tower.

plate 4. Early flushwork in replica windows in Theberton church belfry. Parapet later.

dressings. Internally, within the belfry, the uninterrupted continuity of the wall flintwork behind the blank windows shows that they were not simply blocked redundant belfry openings, but deliberate original decorative features imitating the belfry openings. However, their stonework is still built according to conventional masonry practice; the stones forming their jambs, like those of the belfry openings, are of irregular widths bonding with the surrounding flintwork, and the arches are formed with voussoirs.

The knapped flintwork set flush within conventional stonework in the West Somerton belfry was an innovation that anticipated prototype flushwork such as that on the octagonal belfries of Old Buckenham and Theberton (plate 4) church towers, approximately datable by the Y-tracery of their openings as circa. 1300. As at West Somerton, feigned window shapes on these belfries are infilled with knapped flints and echo the design of the belfry openings, but being two-light with Y-tracery, they posed the question of how replicas of moulded mullions and tracery might be expressed in flush stone and knapped flint. This was resolved by the use of flat, narrow strips of stone for the mullion, branching into curved members of the same width for the inner arcs of the twin arches; similar curved strips instead of voussoirs formed the outer enclosing arch. The jambs, however, were still built with stones of irregular widths rather than strips, suggesting a reluctance to depart completely from traditional practice at this nascent stage of a new technique. This diffidence, though, was soon overcome and narrow stone strips became the norm for the side members of replica windows. Nevertheless, as late as the fifteenth century the original jamb style was still occasionally used, as in the octagonal belfry at Bedingham.

It seems therefore that the replica window was the first motif to be adopted as a subject for flushwork, but an early instance of blind arcading in flushwork on the chancel walls of Wiveton church whose east window with intersecting tracery suggests that it may not be much later than the Theberton and Old Buckenham belfries, shows the development of a single replica feature into a panelling system, and whereas in those early belfry walls knapped flints were used only within the window images, at Wiveton the background walls are also knapped flint. Then, before long, chequer patterns and circular and curvilinear features appear, as shown on St Ethelbert's Gate, Norwich of 1316 (plate 46) and the Gatehouse of Butley Priory, Suffolk of circa 1320, said to be the earliest positively datable examples of flushwork.[1] They show such mastery of the medium as to suggest that when they were built, the craft had advanced appreciably beyond the exploratory standard seen at Old Buckenham and Theberton. In view of the wide geographical spread of these early examples, it is difficult to be certain where the art-form may have originated.

Three-dimensional stone features such as arcading, cresting and crocketting or relief carvings of Gothic-style motifs provided the inspiration for many flushwork designs and were represented by medieval masons as flat patterns. Comparison of the actual belfry opening tracery with its flushwork replicas in the alternate faces of octagonal belfries on towers such as Potter Heigham (plate 60) or Thorpe Abbotts, for example, shows the translation of the former into the latter. Comparably, the repeated motifs in the panelling on the side walls of the porch at Pulham St Mary are flushwork interpretations of the quatrefoil cresting of the parapet, and the flushwork designs of the side parapets of the porches at Southwold (colour plate I) and Ufford (plate 28) are flat representations of the relief stonework patterns of their front parapets.

Despite superficial impressions of structural framing that some flushwork panelling may give, such compositions are purely a non-structural facing on weight-bearing walls. Their stone components contribute little, if anything, to the strength of the flint walls in which they are incorporated; cut from thin slabs, they seem to have been simply mortared on to the rubble flint backing wall, the areas they define then being infilled with knapped flints also mortared to the wall. Often squared in the best work, the infilling flints were closely fitted so that mortar between them was virtually invisible, and where the patterns required, they were precisely worked to the shapes of the enclosing stonework (plate 80).

Tracery motifs, architectural patterns derived from them, and chequerwork were the principal flushwork styles until the emergence towards the middle of the fifteenth century of iconic themes expressed as commemorative or religious symbols, letters, monograms and inscriptions. Such features were often, but by no means always,[2] the products of a different method of construction that was more suited to smaller intricate subjects and seems to have come into use at about the same time: knapped flints were mortared into shallow recesses of the required shapes hollowed out of solid stone blocks that were then incorporated into the structure as prefabricated components. The blocks were square or rectangular and their thickness probably varied according to their location in a building; the regular heights of those used in plinths and buttresses suggest that in such positions they may have made a structural contribution. In any event, flushwork motifs on plinths with weather mouldings above and below them are important aesthetically in providing visual emphasis, with implied solidity, to the base of a tower, porch or other building.

Master masons of churches under construction would have established on-site masons' yards where the stonework for the simpler kinds of flushwork such as panelling or chequerwork would have been worked, but with the development of quite intricate designs, production of prefabricated units may have been centred more on particular workshops. Of these, the Aldryche workshop at North Lopham has been identified as one of the most influential, its style being associated with many churches of the second half of the fifteenth century, mainly in Suffolk and South Norfolk.[3] Other work in the more northern and western parts of Norfolk and in Norwich is stylistically different from the Aldryche mode, and has been suggested as being by a Norwich firm having possible connections with the Cathedral workshop, though the Cathedral itself displays no flushwork.

The flushwork idiom flourished during the fourteenth and fifteenth centuries, but it was in the second half of the fifteenth and during the sixteenth until the Reformation that its greatest splendours were realised. These were times of prosperity in East Anglia, engendered by the wool and cloth trades, and saw the advancement of the art throughout the whole region and the accomplishment of some spectacular masterpieces, especially on the new so-called Wool Churches of the period and on the many new towers, porches, clerestories, buttresses and parapets that were added to existing churches.

plate 5. Incongruous Victorian flushwork on the east end of the south aisle of Elmswell Church.

After the Reformation, church building declined and with it the use of flushwork. Although there are a few later examples such as the chequered chancel wall at Horsham St Faith of 1600 and the 1625 tower at Dalham with its unusual buttress patterns (plate 44), it was not until the nineteenth century that there was a significant revival in the craft, stimulated by a certain amount of new church building and the need for restorations after long neglect. The Victorians showed a diligent capability for fine flushwork, as is demonstrated by the craftsmanship of the re-faced chancel walls of St Michael at Coslany, Norwich and the quality of the blank arcading on the east wall of the chancel at Cromer, but their efforts were not always entirely appropriate – the strident geometrical pattern (plate 5) on the east end of the south aisle of Elmswell church, for instance, does not relate well to the church's architecture nor is it sympathetic to the Gothic style.

From the twentieth century, the most substantial manifestation of flushwork is that on the transepts and eastern additions to the cathedral at Bury St Edmunds begun in 1960 to the design of S.E. Dykes Bower. His extensions respect the Gothic style of the existing church, and most of the flushwork follows the traditional themes of panelling, chequer and quatrefoils. However, the introduction of layered bands of alternating knapped flint and stone on parts of the new work, particularly on the south transept and its turret, represents a divergence from medieval conventions, imposing a horizontal emphasis inimical to the inherent soaring verticality of the building.

Recent restorations of the porches at Woodbridge and Ufford churches, as well as the work at Bury St Edmunds, demonstrate that the skills of creating fine flushwork are still alive, even if some of the restored motifs at Woodbridge may not be strictly authentic. Regrettably though, poor repair work is also sometimes carried out such as the insensitive pointing of the flushwork on the porch at Honington, Suffolk.

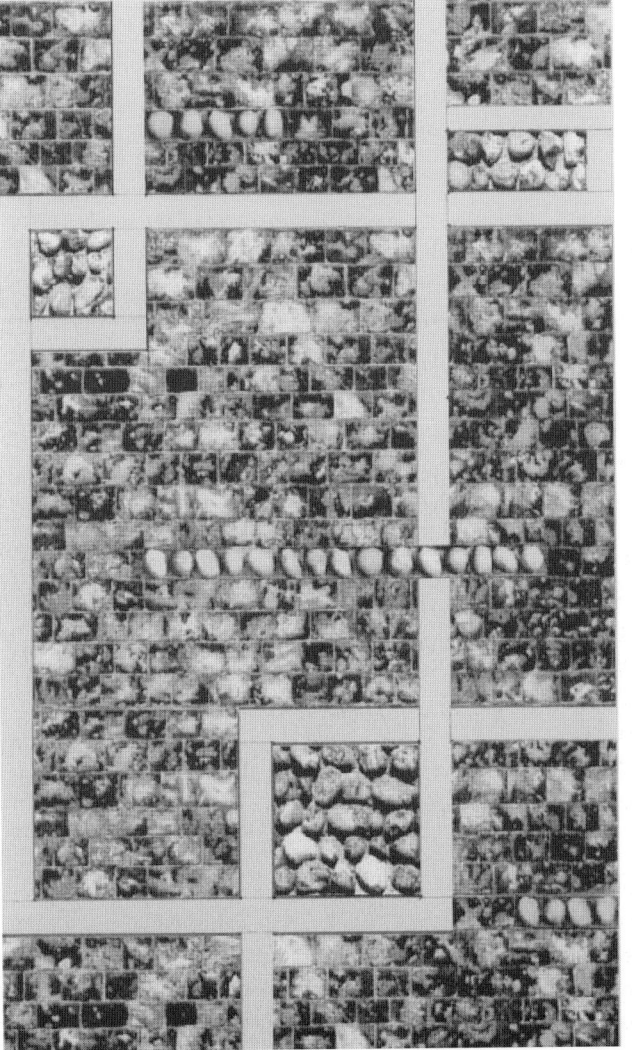

The twentieth-century flushwork mentioned adheres in general to medieval concepts. In the light of its potential as a resource for artistic expression of themes other than conventional medieval ones, it is surprising that, unlike other traditional crafts such as stained glass or mosaics, flushwork does not appear to have been embraced as a medium for modern art. Historically it has been used only on a few buildings other than churches, but flushwork offers abundant scope for innovative interpretation in the secular architecture of today, more particularly in regions where flint is an indigenous building material. As an illustration of its possibilities in contemporary architectue, a hypothetical application of the technique is shown here. In this geometric design for a notional mural panel about 10 feet high, the standard flushwork combination of ashlar stone and squared knapped flints is enlivened by the inclusion of flint cobbles.

Fig 1. A notional abstract composition in flushwork. Collage.

1 N. Pevsner. (revised E. Radcliffe) *The Buildings of England. Suffolk*. Penguin 1974.
2 Emblems above the west door of Coltishall tower and inscriptions on East Tuddenham and Swannington porches are notable exceptions.
3 J. Blatchly and P. Northeast. *Decoding Flint Flushwork*. Suffolk Institute of Archaeology and History. 2005.

CHAPTER TWO

# *Flushwork Themes*

Across the whole field of flushwork a few distinct themes can be identified and these form the basis of virtually all designs in the medium. Some compositions have a single theme and others combine more than one; the main themes are Inset, Imitation windows, Chequer, Emblems, Panelling, Inscriptions and Wavy. In addition to these, there are the analogous crafts derived from flushwork techniques – Brick Flushwork and Relief Flushwork – and another style of flint and stone decoration closely related to Flushwork known as Proudwork. These are considered in the next chapter.

A common usage within some of the flushwork themes, recognisable as a distinctive mode, is the application to horizontal features of continuous sequences of repeated motifs such as the small panels in the plinth of Southwold church and many others, or the quatrefoils in its tower parapet; it was often adopted as a means of emphasising architectural elements such as plinths and parapets. On the south aisle parapet of Coddenham church (plate 64), repetitive small-scale cresting and partially overlapping trefoils alternately inverted fulfil the same purpose though in shorter lengths between the merlons.

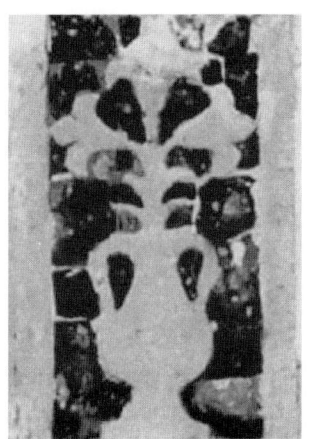

### Inset Flushwork

Most flushwork compositions fully occupy the architectural features or wall areas to which they are applied, but there are arrangements in which individual stone features are inset within a plain flint background, usually knapped flint. The inset elements may be isolated incidents within a plain knapped flint background such as the botonée crosses between the clerestory windows at Wickmere church or they may be separate motifs within larger overall schemes as on the front of the porch of St Andrew's church at Barton Bendish where flush saltire crosses, blank shields and rectangular panels are separately arranged in

plate 6. Inset flushwork emblems in the 'Norwich' style parapet of Griston church tower.

the knapped flint background (colour plate XVIII). Although the inset motifs are usually of flat stone, the rectangular panels on the Barton Bendish porch and several of the lozenge features of the 'Norwich' style parapets (see Chapter 4) have shallow bas-relief carving. Another unusual form of inset flushwork on the Barton Bendish porch is the row of flat stone blank shields with knapped flint between them above the plinth in the rubble flint side walls – reminiscent of a similar dado course on the nave wall of Rickinghall Superior.

Inset motifs, mainly blank shields and lozenge shapes, are typical features of tower parapets of the 'Norwich' style of flushwork, although crossed sword and cross key symbols provide the theme of the 'Norwich' style tower parapet at Griston church (plate 6).

In view of its relative simplicity by comparison with the other flushwork themes, it might be thought that Inset work represented an elementary stage in the development of the art, but that does not appear to be so since it is not confined to early work. The Griston parapet is probably as late as the sixteenth century.

Imitation Windows

The early flushwork replica windows in the belfries of Theberton and Old Buckenham show that not only were they the first subjects of flushwork decoration but they established a theme that was to continue in later work. Feigned windows patterns in Decorated and Perpendicular styles are recurrent features of many of the octagonal belfry stages of circular church towers. Probably contemporary with their towers' circular stages, the fourteenth-century octagonal belfries of some round towers like Theberton or Potter Heigham (plate 60) have flushwork replicas that echo the fourteenth-century styles of the belfry openings, whereas the fifteenth-century belfries that were added to earlier round towers such as at Beachamwell (plate 37) or Bedingham have belfry openings and flushwork replicas of them in Perpendicular styles; all are usually faithful interpretations in flat stone of the three-dimensional tracery of the belfry openings, but the replicas at Poringland (plate 59), there in proudwork (see chapter 3), use a pattern of Decorated tracery different from that of the belfry openings.

The window theme has also been used as a decorative device on other parts of medieval churches; at Ipswich, for example, in the rubble flint west wall of the south aisle of St Margaret's church, knapped flints form the infilling of a large three-light flushwork blank window with intersected tracery, probably of the early fourteenth century, and in later work at Great Witchingham church, a flushwork replica of the Perpendicular clerestory windows (colour plate II) occupies the west end bay of the clerestory. Usually these flushwork window replicas are located in positions where a window might be expected, but on the east end remnant of Little Walsingham Priory church, flushwork designs of two different Decorated window styles, beneath individual crocketted canopy gablets of carved stone (colour plate III), appear on buttresses!

Though not common, circular rose windows interpreted in flushwork made an early appearance, the earliest probably being on St Ethelbert's Gate, Norwich (plate 46). However, those now on the west parapet are restored, but the one in the gable of the east elevation (plate 49) may be the original design. Flushwork rose window replicas also appear in the later tower parapet at Deopham church (plate 55). The tower has angle buttresses that terminate near the top of the belfry stage to form the bases for small polygonal turrets at each corner. These are decorated with flushwork and between them, the battlemented parapet is interrupted in the centre of each face by a triangular gablet. The circular rose window motifs lie within the triangular gablets.

## Chequer Flushwork

Chequer patterns in knapped flint and stone are ubiquitous in East Anglia, but as mentioned earlier, they also occur in other flint areas. In Sussex, the Marlipins at Shoreham is a well-known chequer-faced building of the fourteenth century, and in parts of Wiltshire, for example, chequer is not uncommon on house walls such as at Lake House of about 1580 at Wilsford near Amesbury, a usage quite untypical of East Anglia. In that region though, the pattern can be rather irregular; the stones are not always ashlar and they often slightly overlap in successive courses (plate 7), implying that they are part of the wall structure rather than a facing as in true flushwork. Lapped

plate 7. Lapped chequer pattern of knapped flint and stone on a house wall in Hanging Langford, Wiltshire.

chequer of that kind is rare in East Anglia but can be seen on the tower of St Mary's, Luton, and at Papworth St Agnes church (colour plate VII).

In the areas where they are found outside East Anglia, chequer patterns of stone and knapped flint have not been called flushwork, but in East Anglia chequerwork of these two materials is regarded as part of the flushwork tradition because not only may it be a building's principal decorative theme, as on the fifteenth-century Guildhall and adjacent municipal buildings at King's Lynn, but it often forms part of compositions using other flushwork themes, for example in the clerestory of Woolpit church (colour plate XIII) or on the south porch of Chelmsford cathedral (colour plate XV).

True East Anglian chequer flushwork is a pattern of small, regular, alternating stone and flint squares in a chessboard pattern; their average size is usually about seven to nine inches square but they can be larger as on the parapets of Horringer church and sometimes they are much smaller, about three or four inches square, like those on the porch at Southolt (plate 8) where the flint squares are single flints. The stone squares are slabs of ashlar, accurately cut, and laid with corners touching, thus defining flint squares of the same size as the stone; the flints are always knapped and, in the best work, squared. As well as being laid in chessboard fashion, the squares are often given a diagonal orientation forming a pattern of diamonds, an arrangement sometimes also called lozenge pattern. Nor are the chequer shapes always square: many church buttresses are chequered with vertical rectangles as at Metfield, there are horizontal rectangles on the base of the church tower at Thompson (plate 61) and triangles in the peak of Norwich Guildhall's east gable and on parts of Elveden church.

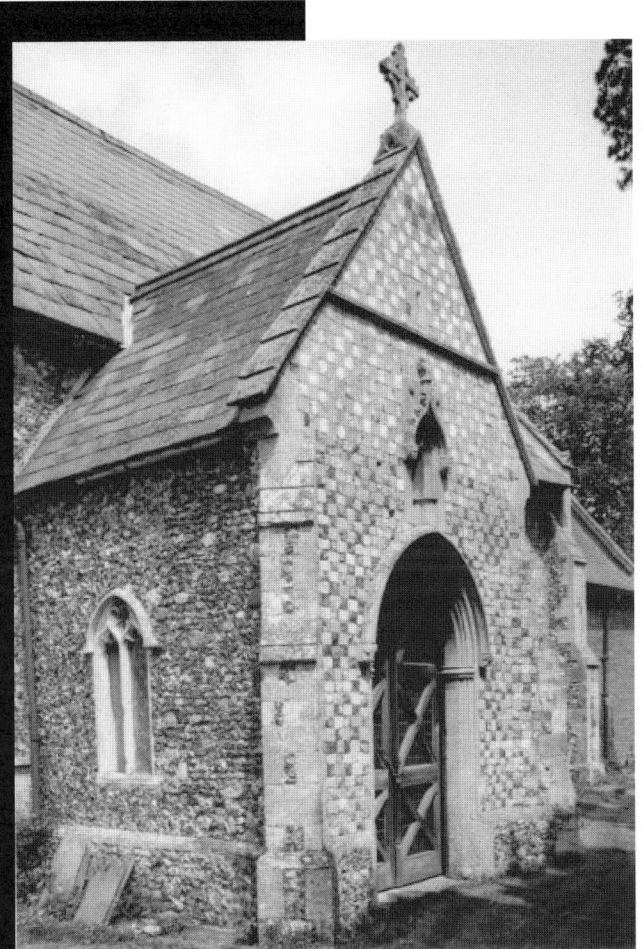

plate 8. Small chequer pattern on the front of Southolt porch.

Straight and diagonal chequers have often been used to decorate the plinths of a church's tower, porch or buttresses, and sometimes, as at Stowlangtoft, the plinth of the whole church. Less common on tower parapets, an unusual arrangement is seen at Starston where the squares are level towards the east but diagonal on the other faces. But chequerwork is most spectacular when it covers large expanses of wall like the east façade of Norwich Guildhall or the frontage of the Guildhall at King's Lynn, faced respectively with diagonal and level squares as are the less well-known porches at Walsham-le-Willows (plate 77) and Southwold (colour plate I) churches, which, though smaller, are no less striking.

When chequerwork entirely covers a wall, its vivid patterning achieves the most telling effect if set against less lively surroundings, for instance when limited to one façade or when its expanse is dominant relative to the architectural detail that it embraces. The King's Lynn municipal buildings make their impact simply as a street frontage without competition from secondary elevations, and at Norwich Guildhall and at the two church porches referred to above the chequer is concentrated on one façade. At St Mary's, Luton, though, the tower has lapped chequer on all its walls, and makes a dramatic statement, but its overall effect is devalued by the profligacy of chequerwork on the rest of the church. The projecting chapels, transepts, buttresses and turret give the church a complicated outline, and the chequer on virtually all their wall surfaces only adds to this restlessness and detracts from architectural clarity.

Chequer patterns depend on contrast between light stone and dark flint and so it is unusual to find instances where light flints have been deliberately selected. In the gable of the chequered porch front at Southolt (plate 8), squares of white knapped flints alternate with warm buff stone squares, reversing and reducing the normal contrasts of light and dark; this is clearly an intentional effect rather than a consequence of ageing or weathering of the flints because, below the gable, the chequerwork has dark flints. Similarly, in the east wall of

Burnham Thorpe church the gable flints are white, while chequer patterns in the same wall lower down use normal black flints.

Conspicuously a characteristic part of the medieval flushwork tradition of East Anglia, chequerwork is not a feature of mainstream Gothic ornament outside the flushwork context. Its formal ordering might suggest a closer affinity with classical architecture, but surprisingly, chequer flushwork, or for that matter flushwork of any kind, does not occur on mature classical buildings and is rare on any post-medieval ones. Notable exceptions though are the Jacobean extension of 1624 to the fifteenth-century Guildhall at King's Lynn referred to above and the church tower at Hopton, where, following the collapse of the top of the tower in the early eighteenth century, a belfry stage with chequered walls (colour plate IV), incorporating modest classical details, replaced the original. It is poised rather uncomfortably on the tower's medieval substructure.

Left to right:

plate 9. Mouchettes, Elmswell.

plate 10. Crowned Marian monogram, Woodbridge.

plate 11. Lily in vase, Grundisburgh.

## Flushwork Emblems

Emblems are those flushwork devices that comprise small self-contained motifs normally not exceeding about three feet or so square, that appear on buildings as individual features, as one of a series, or as elements or focal points within larger compositions. They are frequently used on plinths, parapets and buttresses, and on clerestories and porches.

The material – flint or stone – in which the subject of a flushwork emblem is depicted is not always the same; in some, the emblem's motif is expressed in flint within a stone background and in others it is rendered in stone on a background of flint. It is noticeable that in general, the motifs of tracery-based designs such as trefoils, quatrefoils and mouchettes appear as knapped flint within stone backgrounds (plate 9), whereas representational or symbolic motifs, monograms and initials are usually in stone on flint (plate 10). In a few cases a further motif may be superimposed on the primary motif: an example on the tower at Northwold has a pommée cross of flint in a stone background but the circular extremity of each arm of the flint cross contains a rose in stone with corolla and petals outlined by shallow incisions (plate 14).

Gothic tracery, a purely non-representational decorative theme, was a fruitful source of motifs for emblems during the fourteenth and early fifteenth centuries, and indeed thereafter as well. The ubiquitous trefoils and quatrefoils executed in knapped flint were often used in plinths and below the indents of crenellated parapets (plate 68), and differently configured variants of them with round or pointed lobes or with some of each were artfully adapted to the awkward

Left to right:

plate 12. Crowned sword, Great Cressingham.

plate 13. Catherine wheel, Elmswell.

plate 14. Pommée cross, Northwold.

plate 15. Three of several geometric and star emblems of Hawstead church tower.

# Flushwork Themes 15

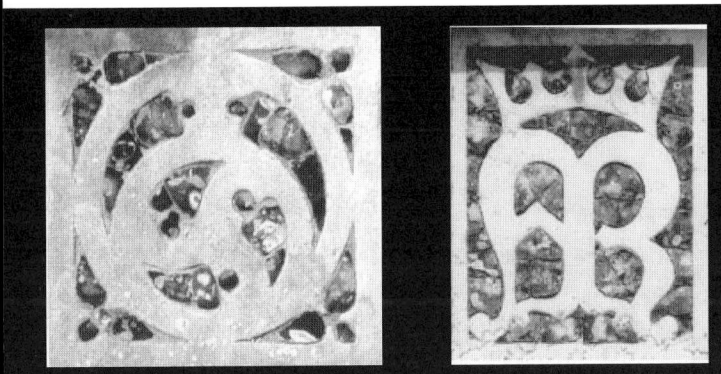
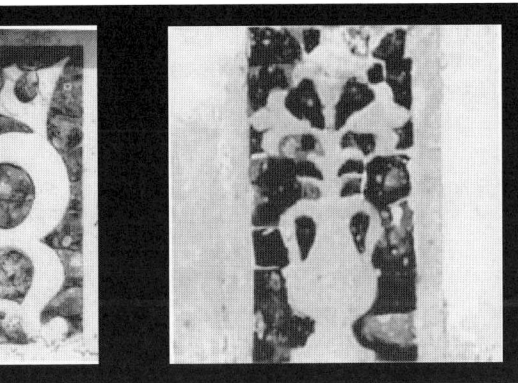

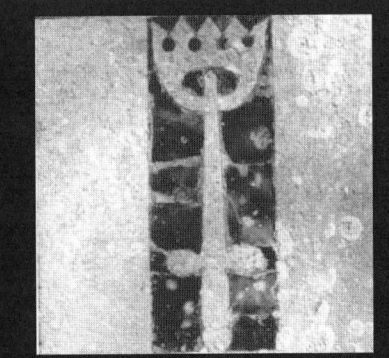

corners of all manner of compositions. Daggers (unequal bi-foils with one rounded lobe and a longer pointed tail), mouchettes (curved variations of the dagger motif) and other foliated shapes derived from tracery play important roles (plate 9). Tracery ideas commonly used are, for example, single quatrefoils in a circle or a square, groups of four quatrefoils, an eccentrically placed roundel within an outer one, each containing other motifs, mouchettes in opposing pairs, or three or more mouchettes within a circle resembling, when seen from a distance, a wheel with curved spokes or when seen from close to, tadpoles. These, separately and in combinations, are typical of the many tracery-inspired emblems to be seen on countless churches throughout East Anglia.

For emblems with descriptive or symbolic meanings, aspects of pre-Reformation theology and legend became favoured subjects. Triangles and circles, usually in threes, represented the Trinity and crowned monograms and initials were used as symbols for Jesus, for Mary, and for the Apostles and Saints. The most common monograms are IHS for Jesus, and, to represent the Blessed Virgin Mary, a Lombardic-style cipher incorporating the letters MARIA superficially resembling an ornate letter M (plate 10). The monogram St, meaning Saint, is also common, usually followed by the initial of a saint. IHS and the Marian monogram, each crowned, are exquisitely depicted in six alternating units above the porch entrance at Rickinghall Superior, and above the great west window of the tower of St Mary's church at Bungay, eight crowned Marian monograms follow the curve of its arch (plate 63). The largest example of this monogram appears in the east face of the tower parapet at Rougham on which a lily in a vase motif, also symbolic of Mary, is twice superimposed. The latter motif, quite rare in flushwork, can also be seen on St John's Abbey Gateway in Colchester and in the clerestory at Grundisburgh (plate 11). As well as crowned initials to identify them, saints may also be celebrated by motifs symbolising their legendary roles or the manner of their martyrdom. Such motifs include a crowned sword (for St Michael) on a porch buttress at Great Cressingham (plate 12), crossed keys (for St Peter) in the Griston tower parapet (plate 6) and on the porch at Kelsale, a wheel with spikes (for St Catherine) at Elmswell (plate 13) and elsewhere and crossed arrows (for St Edmund) at several churches dedicated to him.

Plain shields, perhaps originally painted, are common and are frequently depicted surrounded by lobes or rays, or superimposed on the centre of a quatrefoil or within a cusped circle. Heraldic devices are typical subjects for flushwork emblems; they and uncrowned initials may commemorate individuals, benefactors or the family of a church's patron. Depiction of tools of a trade may be a record of a

## Flushwork Themes

local industry or the occupation of a benefactor or they may represent the insignia of a guild.

Some unusual emblem designs on the tower at Hawstead (plate 15) and others in the clerestory at Cotton exhibit non-figurative patterns that owe little to Gothic tracery or to other precedents. Their geometry of circles, lines and other shapes create abstract patterns in flint and stone which though now unexplained, may have hidden symbolic meanings.

### Flushwork Panelling

Flushwork panelling, also described as arcading or blank niches, is the theme of many of the most spectacular works in the medium. Flushwork panels, comprising vertically-proportioned fields of knapped flint bounded by ashlar stone members, may be arranged in sequences, in pairs or individually on walls or architectural features, as single rows or in superimposed tiers. The flushwork blank arcading on the chancel walls of Wiveton church, mentioned above, suggests that repetitive panelling was an early development. Elsing church tower, which has been dated to the 1330s,[1] provides a relatively early example of the panel motif used singly: it has one flushwork panel in each of the merlons of the crenellated parapet, and a quatrefoil between half-quatrefoils below the indents.

At their simplest, the panels are plain knapped flint rectangles as in the clerestory at Wortham (plate 39) or on the porch at Market Weston (plate 74), where on the stone above the panels, shallow sinkings barely a quarter of an inch deep delineate foliated shapes. Those, and similar ones on the porches at Finningham (plate 16) and Thornham Magna, and at a few other churches (Appendix C) are clearly part of the original designs, but in some cases they are probably simply a cheap repair of proper flushwork. Outside the flushwork context, similar shallow sinkings in stonework are paralleled by the crowned letters over the north porch entry at Wickham Skeith, shields in the parapet of Little Waldingfield tower (plate 72) and isolated details on the porch at Metfield (plate 75).

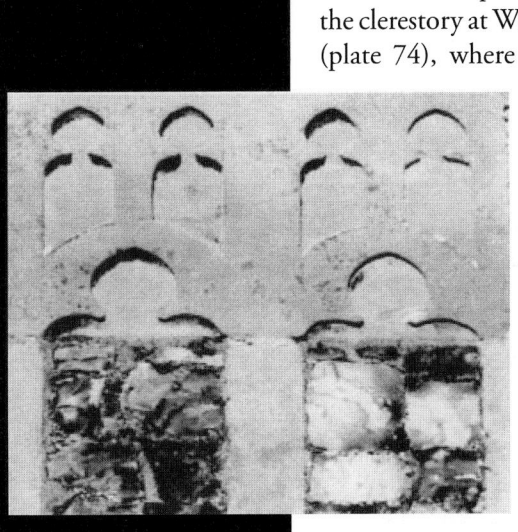

plate 16. Shallow sunk stone heads to rectangular knapped flint panels on Finningham porch. The apparent variation in depth of some of the sinkings in the photograph is an optical illusion arising from uneven dark weather staining.

Plain rectangular panelling is not widespread but is common enough to represent a distinct trend, but in most flushwork panelling schemes, the stonework at the head of each flint-filled panel is shaped as a foliated arch. This arch may be trefoiled with a round (plate 20) or pointed centre

18  *Flint Flushwork*

plate 17. Trefoiled panels.

plate 18. Cinquefoiled panels.

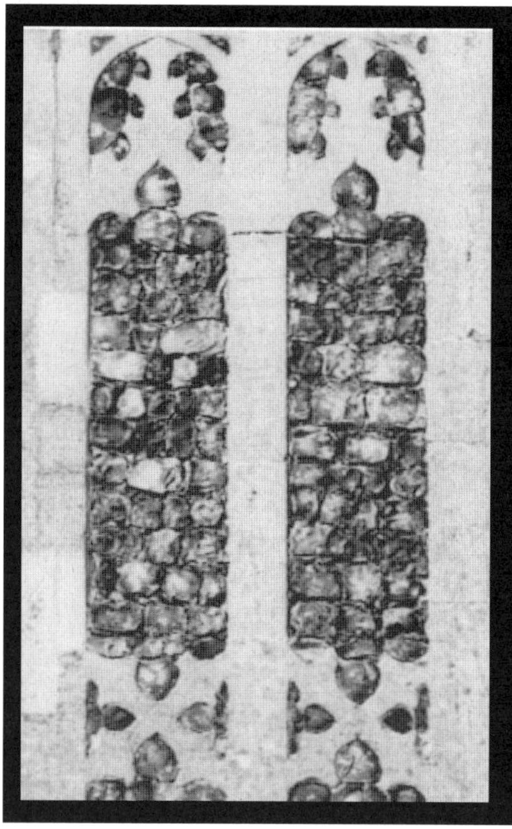

plate 19. Canopied panels

plate 20. Supermullioned panels.

Flushwork Themes 19

plate 21. Straight-headed    plate 22. Castellated    plate 23. Canopy-headed
Where panels are tiered the stone heads of the lower panels may be straight, castellated or canopied.

plate 24. Halesworth porch. Paired panels in middle flushwork band.

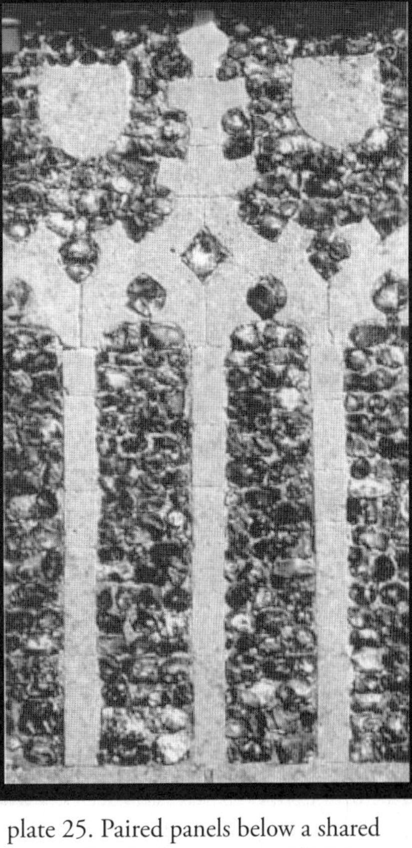

plate 25. Paired panels below a shared canopy-head with crocketted finial.

lobe (plate 17), cinquefoiled (plate 18), or round-headed enclosing a small crocketted and finialled canopy motif (plate 19); in the foliated types, the stonework at the arch apex may rise as a supermullion into the area above the panel, dividing it into two mouchette shapes or narrower sub-panels (plate 20). Where panels are tiered, the top of the arch stonework of a lower panel that forms the base of the one above it is usually level (plate 21), castellated (plate 22) or canopied (plate 23), but in some cases, as on the Bressingham clerestory, repetitions of the lower panel's foliation pattern mirrored above and alongside it create a cross-shaped motif between the panels (plate 19). This motif or variations of it have also been used as independent emblems. A richer and larger-scale effect was achieved by pairing two panels beneath a shared head as in the middle band of panelling on Halesworth porch (plate 24), but this detail was more usually developed into a canopy head with a crocketted finial (plate 25), as on porches at Glemsford and Chelmsford (colour plate XV), on clerestories at Cavendish (colour plate XIV) and Long Melford and on the Gatehouses of St Osyth's Priory and St John's Abbey, Colchester.

Panelling is a principal theme on the majority of buildings that have flushwork decoration and, adapting easily to the proportions of any feature whether the narrow vertical face of a buttress or a long horizontal plinth, panels are frequently used singly, in pairs or sequences to embellish church buttresses, parapets, plinths and dado friezes. But the greatest tours de force of flushwork panelling are to be seen in the more expansive compositions that cover entire walls at certain East Anglian churches such as the south aisle and chancel of St Michael at Coslany in Norwich (plate 43) or the towers of Redenhall (colour plate XI), Eye and Laxfield, reviewed in the next chapter.

plate 26. Lombardic inscription on Swannington church porch.

plate 27. Part of the Gothic script inscription on Stratford St Mary church.

INSCRIPTIONS

Inscriptions in Lombardic or Gothic script, executed in flushwork may be invocations, praise, or dedications, and often they commemorate benefactors or solicit prayers for their souls, but whatever may be the meaning of an inscription and whether or not it is intelligible, its lettering can make an effective form of linear ornament. Indeed, greater clarity of wording may tend to reduce its impact as decoration, as the legends in Roman style lettering on the tower parapet at Dalham (plate 44) seem to show when compared with medieval examples of Lombardic or Gothic scripts. Latin wording or archaic English spellings and unfamiliar letter forms of many of these inscriptions may seem bewildering to some who contemplate them today, but perhaps no more so than to the majority of a population who at the time that the lettering was carved would have been illiterate.

Although common as individual letters in emblems, Lombardic characters are used in only a few inscriptions. Those over the entrance arches of the porches at Swannington (plate 26) and East Tuddenham (colour plate V) and above the arch of the west window of Southwold church tower (plate 76) are the finest examples – at the latter two, each letter is crowned. On the east end of the chancel at Blythborough, individual crowned Lombardic letters occupying seperate flushwork squares could be a coded indication that they are the initial letters of words, and in fact they have been deciphered as the initial letters of a re-dedication of the chancel.[2]

The characters of Gothic script carved in stone against a background of black knapped flint unquestionably yield the most richly decorative form of flushwork calligraphy. Also known as black-letter, the alternative appellation 'Gothic' for this script is preferable when used in the flushwork context because in such work the letters are light in tone against their black background. Nowhere is Gothic script more telling than on the plinth of the north aisle and chapel at

Stratford St Mary church (plate 27). Like the mouldings of the plinth, the lettering continues around projecting buttresses thus maintaining an uninterrupted band of enrichment along the east and north walls. It is interesting, though, that in these inscriptions and in others in this script elsewhere, Lombardic characters are sometimes used for the initial letter of a word.

Lesser displays appear in commemorative panels in the tower parapets at Rougham and Badwell Ash, but at several other churches, notably Helmingham, Garboldisham and Great Waldingfield among others, the flint filling of otherwise surviving inscriptions has been lost. At Botesdale, a three-line inscription within ashlar stonework over the north door has been interrupted by the insertion of a later window.

Wavy Flushwork

This form of flushwork usually provides a supporting role as part of other compositions rather than as a principal theme, and is not very common. It can take the form of sinuous strips interweaving between circular emblems, as in the frieze of Rougham tower parapet, or of undulating stone bands between foliated flint shapes, as on the side parapets of the porches at Ufford (plate 28) and Blyford. Twining plant stems in stone produce the same general effect, though those in the north clerestory parapet at Coddenham, perhaps the only surviving examples of that particular pattern, have, sadly, lost their knapped flint infillings.

plate 28. Relief wavy ornament of the front parapet interpreted as flushwork in the side parapets of Ufford church.

1  N. Pevsner and B. Wilson. *The Buildings of England. Norfolk 2: North-West and South*. Penguin 1999.
2  J. Blatchly and P. Northeast, op. cit.

CHAPTER THREE

# Themes with Affinity to Flushwork

### BRICK FLUSHWORK

Brick flushwork is similar to the normal freestone kind except that the frameworks which enclose the knapped flint are formed in brick. By comparison with stone which could be cut from relatively large pieces into quite intricate shapes, bricks were only available as small units – 9½" x 4¾" x 2" was a typical medieval brick size – and were less amenable to being formed into complex patterns; consequently, brick flushwork designs are limited to simple patterns. The width of framing members follows from the width or thickness of the bricks and the only elaborations are simple foliations at the tops of the panels formed with specially moulded bricks.

plate 29. Brick flushwork window on St Benedict's tower, Norwich.

There are only a few examples of brick flushwork (Appendix B), and most date from the fifteenth century. Three brick porches of this period have flushwork panelling: Great Ashfield has panelling on the front wall and the bases of the side walls, Great Bealings has a panelled base, and Ixworth Thorpe has panelling on buttresses and side parapets (colour plate VI). All have narrow panels, little more than the width of half a brick, with simple foliated heads of moulded bricks, formed in a slightly different way in each case. The flint porch at Great Barton has a base of brick flushwork, again comprising narrow panels with foliated heads of moulded brick, and on a knapped flint vestry at Gosbeck, rebuilt in the 1840s, the brick flushwork parapet has wider panels with plain heads.

In brick chequer flushwork, the size of the squares derives from brick sizes. Five-inch squares on the porch at Hardwick with single knapped flints between are equivalent to half a brick; on the tower parapet at Saxlingham the squares are one-brick size and on New Buckenham tower parapet, one and a half. By contrast, the rectangular brick and flint chequer pattern covering the whole of the tower of Wheatacre church has brick panels nearly three feet wide by about two feet high with knapped flint panels of the same size, but can this be considered as flushwork?

One-brick-size chequer flushwork with light bricks and dark flint can be seen on the fourteenth-century chancel at Lawford (colour plate X) and with red bricks and light flints on the front of Weybourne church porch.

Rivalling the chequered wall on Lawford chancel as the earliest example of any form of brick flushwork are the dummy windows formed with medieval bricks within the knapped flint of the octagonal belfry of the enduring round tower of St Benedict's church in Norwich (plate 29), all that survives of the church destroyed in an air raid in 1942. They are of Y-tracery pattern like the belfry openings and suggest an early fourteenth-century date. At Old Catton, a later octagonal belfry on the round tower, probably of the sixteenth century, also has brick flushwork dummy windows – they copy the Perpendicular panel tracery of the belfry openings.

The tower parapet of Caistor St Edmund church has simple panelling of brick flushwork of the late fifteenth or early sixteenth centuries and there is similar work in the later nineteenth-century parapets of the towers at Roughton and Ardleigh (plate 79). At Ringsfield, the medieval tower has a seventeenth-century parapet decorated with two-stage brick flushwork panelling in which the upper and lower panels are staggered relative to each other, rather in the manner of diaper brickwork. True diaper or lozenge patterns, formed by a lattice of brick headers staggered by the width of half a brick relative to those in adjacent courses occur on the knapped flint clerestory walls of Great Witchingham church (colour plate II) and on a few other later church and secular buildings, some within as-found flintwork.

Flushwork with Unknapped Flints

This practice is similar to true flushwork except that the flint infilling within the freestone frameworks is not knapped but may instead be cobbles or rubble with the result that the uneven flints, though notionally level with the stone surfaces, cannot be flush with them. The general effect though, is similar to flushwork as may be seen on plate 30. Cobble flints in the panel infillings in the merlon zones, alternating with chequer squares of stone and knapped flint below the indents, on the tower parapet at Dickleburgh.

the tower parapet at Little Waldingfield (plate 72) where panels of rubble flint alternate with knapped panels between the stone strips. When the rubble flint infilling is similar in colour to the stone, the visual contrast between the two materials depends more on the textural difference between them.

The most impressive example of unknapped flushwork, which is not a common technique in East Anglia, is seen in the nineteenth-century church at Papworth St Agnes (colour plate VII) where all the walls of church and tower are built in a lapped chequer. In these walls, the alternating spaces between the ashlar stone elements are filled with cobbly erratics and flints, with the erratics predominating; this mixture of cobbly erratics and flints is typical of the walls of churches built on the boulder clays on the western edge of East Anglia.

Contorted nodules and roughly cleft flints are the ingredients of the infilling of the trefoiled panels on the base of the medieval tower of Horham church (plate 69). This appears to be original work rather than a repair and makes a surprising contrast with the high-quality genuine flushwork on the tower parapet, which, however may be later.

The parapet of Sudbourne church tower, probably a Victorian restoration, typifies simple unknapped flushwork panelling. It has a pattern of foliated panels infilled with well-selected cobble flints whose yellow-brown hues blend closely with the warm buff stonework of the panelling framework. A similar tonal harmony is seen in the nineteenth-century gable of the sixteenth-century porch at Salcott church (colour plate VIII) where the panel infillings are of knapped and rubble flints mixed with septaria.

The unusual design of the decoration on the parapet of the fourteenth-century tower of Dickleburgh church (plate 30) is probably unique and may be later than the tower structure. Wide trefoiled panels faced with flint cobbles alternate with large squares containing nine smaller squares of conventional chequer flushwork, and as there are no stone bands separating the panels from the chequer squares, the knapped flints of the chequer flushwork are contiguous with the cobbles of the trefoiled panels; it is therefore only the difference of colour and texture between the two types of flint that prevents a rather awkward visual merging of the cobble panels and the chequer squares.

CARSTONE FLUSHWORK

This is a rare variation in whch the flush infill material within the stonework patterns is carstone instead of the more normal knapped flint. An instance, probably unique, occurs at Sandringham church where, on the porch and tower parapet, small carstone slips or brickettes are used. They are characteristic of buildings in the locality, as seen in the walls of the church itself.

PROUDWORK

Proudwork and flushwork both seem to have originated in the early fourteenth century, but there is no certainty as to which came first. The spandrels of squared knapped flint enclosed by raised stone mouldings on the early fourteenth-century south aisle of Bottisham

plate 31. Proudwork blank windows on the east front of Burnham Norton Friary Gatehouse.

church (plate 83) must be one of the first uses of knapped flint as recessed infilling within moulded stonework and can be seen as a precursor of proudwork; it could therefore be argued that recessing of knapped flint infilling behind window mullions and tracery, as in the simulated windows in the restored front and rear walls (plate 31) of Burnham Norton Friary Gatehouse, if they faithfully represent the original, was a logical development from the early flushwork precursor at West Somerton described earlier (plate 3), and that the step towards flat stone members as at Theberton (plate 4) and Old Buckenham followed.

Proudwork, as its name implies, is not a form of flushwork although it is often incorrectly so described. Like flushwork though, it is a decorative technique combining the use of knapped flint and freestone, but the stone elements of the patterns stand proud from the knapped flint and consequently become the dominant elements of the composition. The distinction between the two techniques can be clearly seen on the north clerestory of Wymondham Abbey where the two easternmost bays are decorated with proudwork (plate 62) while the others are in flushwork.

Although by no means a rarity, proudwork never became as universally established as flushwork; about fifty or so churches have proudwork features of some kind (Appendix A). It mostly occurs as panelling, as on the plinths of the tower at Blakeney and the nave at

plate 32. Proudwork panels and quatrefoils on the tower parapet of North Tuddenham church.

Weasenham St Peter or on buttresses as at Great Massingham (plate 56) and Lowestoft, but there are also quatrefoils of proudwork between the panels in the tower parapets at North Tuddenham (plate 32), Shipdham and Mattishall. Feigned windows occur in the clerestory at Northwold, a sham bay window disguises a fireplace at Gipping, and the octagonal belfry stages of the round towers at Bylaugh, Poringland (plate 59), Quidenham and Stanford have two-light proudwork window replicas. Unusually, the tracery of the proudwork replicas at Poringland is a different pattern from that of the belfry openings.

On the front of the porch at Southwold, within the knapped flint of the proudwork panels defined by stone mouldings, there are stone motifs in the form of small castellated panel heads set flush with the flint. Flushwork within proudwork is therefore created – a harmonious union of the two techniques in one work.

Normally the stonework members in proudwork are worked to moulded profiles comparable to window tracery sections and stand well proud of the flintwork, but in a few cases they have peculiarly flat faces with bevelled edges and a relatively smaller projection. This type can be seen on the church tower parapets at North Creake, North Elmham and Castle Acre, and on the two eastern bays of the north clerestory at Wymondham (plate 62).

Occasionally a variation is found where the knapped flint infill is recessed by as little as a quarter of an inch from flat stonework members as used in normal flushwork; however, since the flint recession is so small and the stone members are unmoulded, this peculiarity should perhaps be regarded as deviant flushwork rather than proudwork. It has been noticed on the south porch at Brome (plate 33) and on the tower parapets at Barton Turf, Hickling and Haveringland.

plate 33. Shallow recession of knapped flint infilling of panels on the front of the south porch at Brome.

CHAPTER FOUR

# The Architectural Setting

## TOWER PARAPETS

The parapet is the crowning glory of a church tower and however austere the rest of the church exterior may be, the top of the tower has usually been given some form of embellishment. Parapets may be single-stage or two-stage and customarily terminate with crenellations, either battlemented or stepped. Most conform to one of the four basic formats shown diagrammatically on page 30, although their detail may vary and there are a few that do not follow these patterns. For convenience of reference, the four types have been given the notations shown in figure 2.

Flushwork or proudwork of some kind provides the parapet decoration of over 250 church towers in East Anglia and all styles of flushwork have been used. Panelling designs are most common, often with emblems in the shallower spaces below the indents of the crenellations. Chequer patterns as the main theme on tower parapets are relatively few: Starston, as mentioned on page 12, has chequer squares set straight and diagonally on different faces of the tower, on Horringer parapet the squares are exceptionally large and at Little Thurlow the 'squares' have slightly oblong proportions.

Of the single-stage tower parapets, those at Kersey and Ringland show greater originality and intricacy than average. At Kersey (colour plate IX) the battlemented parapet has cinquefoiled panels in both merlons and indents, each containing a finialled quatrefoil at the base, and in the stepped parapet at Ringland, quite elaborate double and triple stages of foliation fill the tops of the panels, with foliated emblems below the indents. Helmingham and Horham have lavish panelling and emblems in their stepped parapets and are so similar as to suggest the hand of the same mason.

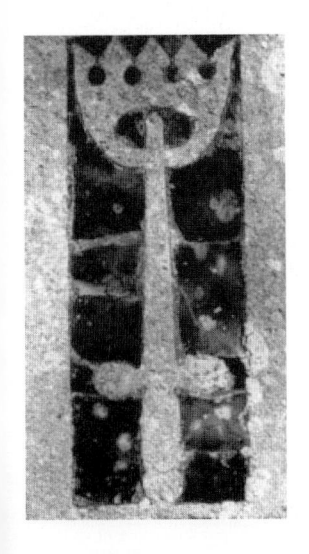

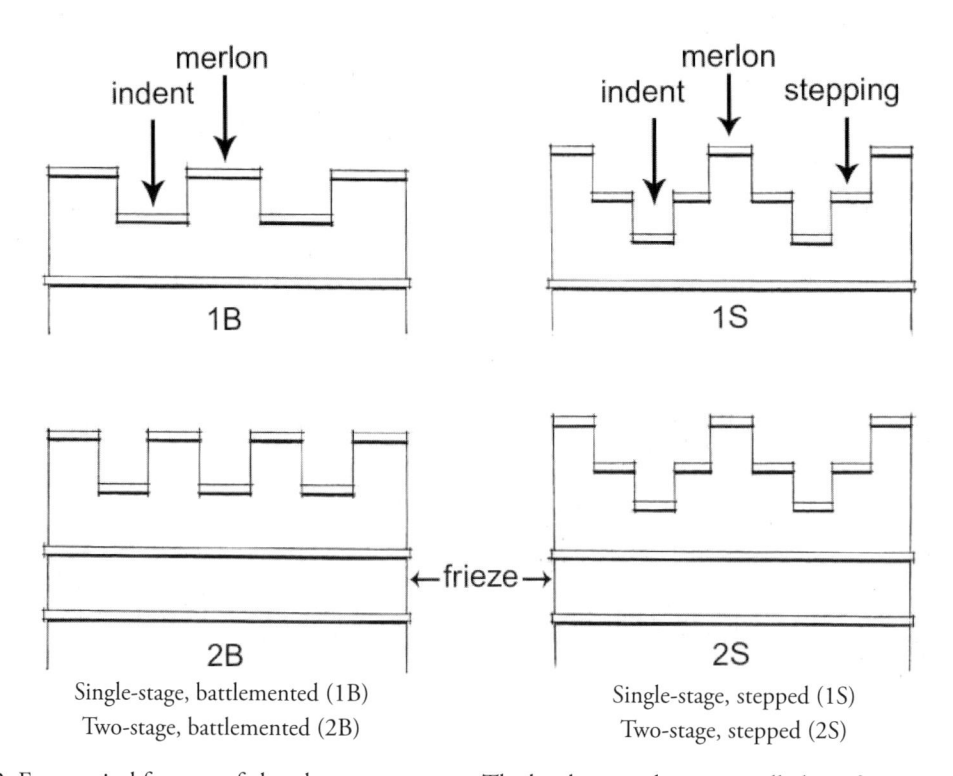

fig 2. Four typical formats of church tower parapets. The battlemented types usually have five or seven, sometimes nine, zones on each face, and the stepped types nine.

Single-stage, battlemented (1B)
Two-stage, battlemented (2B)
Single-stage, stepped (1S)
Two-stage, stepped (2S)

The battlemented parapet of Woodbridge tower must be the most showy of the two-stage types, although much of its detail is too small to be fully appreciated from the ground: it has large and small emblems and panelling in the top stage, and hexafoiled triangles between single rows of diagonal chequer in the frieze. Rivalling the detail of the Woodbridge parapet, those at Rougham and Great Barton (colour plate XVI) rank among the finest of the stepped types.

Brick flushwork decorates a few tower parapets – as medieval chequerwork at Saxlingham Nethergate and New Buckenham, as medieval panelling at Caistor St Edmund, in modern restorations at Ardleigh (plate 79) and Roughton, and as staggered panels at Ringsfield.

By comparison with the referential designs of the turreted tower parapets at Deopham (plate 55) and Redenhall, the unorthodox tower parapet and stair turret at Earls Colne is fulsome and oppressive, with its heavy relief carvings on two sides and excessively star-spangled flushwork.

An unorthodox, rather restrained flushwork style is a feature of the tower parapets of a few city churches in Norwich: St Clement's

plate 34. Lattice pattern flushwork on the tower parapet at Althorne.

(plate 58), St George's Colegate, St George's Tombland and St John-le-Sepulchre all have single-stage battlemented parapets faced with knapped flint that are simply divided into five plain rectangular zones by vertical flush stone strips coinciding with the spacing of the crenellations. Within these zones, independent stone motifs are inset consisting mainly of small blank shields and lozenge shapes; the lozenges are often carved in shallow relief, depicting shields or other symbols. Church tower parapets with this 'Norwich' style flushwork (see Appendix D) are also found in the nearby villages of Blofield, North Burlingham and Coltishall and in a few others further afield, for example at Griston (plate 6). Except for the parapet at Northrepps which is stepped, all are battlemented and divided into five zones like those in Norwich and most have motifs that are generally similar to the Norwich towers.

Division by stone strips into zones corresponding with the crenellations in the manner of the 'Norwich' style also occurs on the unusual triple-stepped tower parapet of Little Waldingfield church (plate 72). It has square stone panels below the two indents but the other zones are faced alternately with knapped and rubble flints without inset stone motifs. Although this tower may be earlier than most of those with 'Norwich' style flushwork, it is perhaps unlikely to be a prototype for the style.

Several churches with round towers have flushwork on their tower parapets. Those on the early towers of Roughton and Haveringland were nineteenth-century additions; others, like Wickmere, may have been an original part of the circular tower, while those on contemporary or added octagonal belfries as at Potter Heigham (plate 60) and Taverham respectively are probably the same age as the belfries. All are battlemented and single-stage, and typically their flushwork theme is panelling with emblems below the indents in some cases. Hales is an exception, having an uncrenellated circular parapet with chequer flushwork.

One tower parapet calls for special mention because of its unique flushwork. The single-stage battlemented parapet at Althorne in Essex (plate 34) has a pattern in which a lattice of stone strips encloses an unbroken pattern of knapped flint diamond shapes, entirely covering merlon and indent zones. The only comparable example of this style

plate 35. Unequal panel widths on the east side of Redenhall church tower.

is on the east end of Barsham church (frontispiece), but the Althorne parapet, if contemporary with its tower, may be the earlier.

## Church Towers

Tower bases with flushwork decoration are almost as common as flushwork parapets and the same themes are employed, i.e. panelling as at Southwold and countless others, chequer as at Stowlangtoft, and emblems as at Woodbridge; occasionally, as at Happisburgh, there is proudwork. Curiously, the plinth of Scarning tower has proudwork panelling on the south and west sides and flushwork on the north.

Some fifty or so square church towers have flushwork on parts of their superstructure other than parapets and plinths, but nowhere does it make such a spectacular display as on the architecturally similar towers of Redenhall (colour plate XI), Eye and Laxfield mentioned above. Flushwork covers the full height of the west fronts in panelling bands of different heights that correspond with the tower's architectural features. The bands are alternately of single and double-width panels, the panel heads of the wider ones being supermullioned and thus creating the narrower panels of the band above. The pattern established by the correlation of the bands forms the main theme of these geometrical compositions, and an intriguing design problem is revealed in the flushwork of the east face of Redenhall's tower (plate 35). Because the stair turret at the south-east corner is larger than the polygonal north-east buttress, the widths of the wall spaces each side of the central belfry opening are different.

plate 36. Flushwork dado on Worstead church tower.

They have both, however, been divided into three panels, those on the left of the opening being noticeably narrower than those on the right. Above these, the panels of the next panelling band (which embraces the arch of the belfry opening), being half the width of the ones below also produce different panel widths on each side of the arch and this is particularly noticeable where they meet above its apex. It is odd that the belfry opening was not located centrally between turret and buttress, thus aligning symmetrically with the parapet above and obviating the unequal panel widths.

Only a few other towers have flushwork of note on their main stages. St Lawrence's church tower in the urban setting of Dial Lane, Ipswich, makes a memorable spectacle (colour plate XII). Opulent flushwork on its two upper stages, rebuilt in 1882, includes diagonal chequer, panelling and circular emblems, and the richness of effect is enhanced by bands of stone carving between the stages and the fine stepped openwork parapet. However, whereas the lower stages of the tower and their buttresses are of traditional flint construction, polygonal ashlar quoins and other decorated stonework on the two upper stages impart to them an entirely different character; they create the effect of a stone structure because the only visible flint is the knapped flint in the flushwork decoration.

plate 37. Flushwork window replica in the octagonal belfry stage of the round tower at Beachamwell church.

The tower of St Stephen's, Norwich, also has a stone upper stage. Separated by a flushwork frieze of quatrefoils from the black knapped flint walls of the lower stage, the ashlar upper walls have flushwork feigned windows flanking the belfry openings, with a lozenge and two circles of knapped flint above.

The west front of Southwold tower presents an imposing display of flushwork themes: panelling with some unusual details each side of the west doorway and window and also on the buttresses, a large area of chequer above the window and, as mentioned on page 21, the inscription in crowned Lombardic letters following the curves of the window arch.

Flushwork on the west fronts of other towers is less ambitious, the most usual schemes being a frieze of emblems over the west doorway as at Northwold, or a group of panels flanking the west doorway or window as at Hilborough or Kersey. Woodbridge and Coltishall towers have both. Exceptionally, at Worstead (plate 36), a dado of intersecting flushwork panelling is extended across the north and south walls of tower and buttresses.

The plinths and buttresses of the towers of some of the 'wool' churches of the fifteenth and sixteenth centuries provide the settings for prolific displays of flushwork emblems. The towers of Elmswell, Northwold, Garboldisham, Badwell Ash and Hawstead churches are particularly notable for the numbers of their emblems and the variety of the subjects that they express; by contrast though, repetition takes the place of variety on the tower at Thrandeston where the selfsame rather unusual emblem design (plate 52) is repeated ten times in the plinths of each wall and on the buttresses, and above them in the west wall there is a row of identical rayed shields.

About 170 churches in East Anglia have round towers still standing, but since many of them were built before its invention, flushwork only appears in a few of the later medieval ones, Ilketshall St Andrew, for example, and in the upper parts of the older towers that have been added or rebuilt. On most of the sixty or so octagonal belfry stages on circular towers, the belfry openings are located in the cardinal faces and about a quarter of those have, in their diagonal faces, flushwork replicas echoing their two-light window pattern. Examples in Perpendicular style can be seen at Bedingham and Beachamwell (plate 37). As mentioned earlier, the replica windows have in a few cases been carried out in proudwork. No flushwork themes other than replica windows seem to have been used on the diagonal faces of these octagonal belfry stages except on the tower at Breckles (plate 54) where they are patterned entirely with chequer flushwork.

### Porches

In the prosperous years of the later middle ages, new porches were added to many East Anglian churches and about 180 display some flushwork, even if only on plinths or buttresses. Most are single-storey and conform to one basic architectural design having a front entrance arch, niche or niches above (usually), and single windows in the side walls. They may be parapetted (colour plate I) or gabled (plate 65) with, at the front corners, either diagonal buttresses (a single buttress meeting the corner diagonally) or angle buttresses (one on each wall meeting the corner at right-angles). Two-storied porches generally follow the same architectural form as the single-storey ones except that the wall above the entrance arch contains a window or windows to light the upper room. On both single- and two-storey porches,

plate 38. Well proportioned flushwork panelling on the angle-butressed porch front at Hitcham.

diagonal buttresses are much more common than the angle type, and so are parapetted fronts; the parapets are usually battlemented and often continued along the side walls.

Despite the general similarity of the architecture of the porches, the flushwork shows a fascinating range of variation in its detail; emblems and panelling are the most common themes, the emblems usually in plinths and parapets, with the panelling on the fronts.

The porch was a favourite canvas on which a church benefactor could display and lavish his riches, and so showmanship and exuberance of expression sometimes seemed to be more prized than architectural integrity and restraint. The porch front at Kersey (plate 71), for instance, impressive though it may be for its craftsmanship and the variety of its motifs, has certain design weaknesses: the three-stage base decorated with different themes and extending to three-quarters of the height of the archway jambs gives uncomfortable proportions and the diagonal chequerwork of the parapet, aligned to the pitch of the roof, relates clumsily with the vertical stonework of the corner pinnacles and parapet crenellations. The porch front at Ixworth also illustrates how poorly-considered flushwork can detract from a design: a band of panelling over the entrance bears no relationship to the shape of the wall space it occupies.

Of all the flushwork porches, the finest can be identified as those where the flushwork compositions harmonise so naturally with the architectural elements that they are comprehended as features of a coherent design rather than simply as superficial finery. Porches at Huntingfield, Badwell Ash or Great Bromley (plate 81) of the type with diagonal buttresses and those at Hitcham (plate 38) or Felsham with angle buttresses are beautiful single-storey designs which admirably demonstrate this quality. Of the two-storey porches, those at Redenhall (with diagonal buttresses) and Lowestoft (with angle buttresses) also have well-integrated flushwork.

Apart from plinths and parapets, a few porches have flushwork on their side walls; Southwold (colour plate I) and Woolpit have chequer squares; Woodbridge, Ufford, Glemsford, Pulham St Mary, Preston, and one or two others have panelling on one or both sides. Chelmsford has both and is unique in having, below the parapet, a row of emblems between which there are panels of rich red brick each with a lozenge motif in blue bricks (colour plate XV).

Brick flushwork panelling decorates the front of the porch at Great Ashfield and at Weybourne the flushwork on the porch gable is brick chequer. Elsewhere a few other porches have small areas of brick flushwork (see Appendix B).

plate 39. Two-stage clerestory with emblems and rectangular panels below the string course at Wortham.

## Clerestories

The clerestory walls of about thirty or so East Anglian churches are decorated with flushwork and these are of two types. In two-stage clerestories the spaces between the windows are bisected by a stone string course running between the windows; the string course is a horizontal extension of the window hoodmoulds and is normally located at about the level of the bottom of window tracery thereby giving the lower stage taller proportions than the upper. In single-stage clerestories the spaces between the windows are uninterrupted by a string course.

Of the few single-stage clerestories with flushwork, those at Cavendish (colour plate XIV) and Long Melford, less than four miles away, in particular stand out. Almost identical architecturally except for the closer spacing at Long Melford of the lofty three-light windows, both have between the windows paired flushwork panels below a common traceried and crocketted head that coincides with the level of the window tracery. At their mid-height, the transome detail of the window lights is echoed in the flushwork panels, thus establishing a harmonious unity between fenestration and flushwork.

Other single-stage clerestories include New Buckenham which has panelling between the windows up to arch level and alternating brick and flint voussoirs in the window arches, Stalham and Wickmere with inset features between the windows, Rackheath with short groups of panels only at each end and Tunstead which has flushwork blank arcading for the full length of its long low windowless clerestory.

Opposite.
plate 40. Two stage clerestory with panelling above and below the string course at Earl Stonham.

Some two-stage clerestories have flushwork only below the string course, with panelling at Woodbridge and Stratford St Mary, emblems at Walsham-le-Willows and both at Wortham (plate 39). Flushwork above and below the string course occurs as panelling at Great Bromley and Earl Stonham (plate 40), and as emblems at Bacton. Flushwork in the upper stage only of a clerestory is rare: an example at Cotton has emblems above the string course.

Voussoir patterns using rich red bricks instead of stone enliven the arches of many clerestory windows and where they are associated with flushwork, the effect is cheerfully colourful. Several clerestories display this combination, notably Cotton, Bacton and Walsham-le-Willows. At Wortham (plate 39), slightly wider window spacing allows the brick arch voussoirs to continue down to the string course level, enhancing their effect.

The flushwork on most clerestories is displayed between the windows, but the south clerestory at Rattlesden is noteworthy for the distinctive flushwork of its parapet (plate 41). The subjects of its sixteen emblems below the indents, mainly symbols of the apostles, are finely delineated by unusually slender stonework in a style not seen elsewhere, but between the indents, the stonework members of paired panels in the merlons, alternately of canopied or supermullion patterns, are of normal flushwork proportions.

The most unexpected flushwork clerestory must surely be the one on St Wendreda's church at March. Situated in the Cambridgeshire fens some distance from flint and flushwork country, this church is of limestone and has a late medieval two-stage clerestory; on the south side, the clerestory is built of stone rubble up to the level of the string course but above this, the wall is knapped flint, with brick voussoirs in the window arches and single flushwork emblems between the

plate 41. Slender stonework in emblems on the clerestory parapet of Rattlesden church nave.

plate 42. Flushwork on the east end of Mutford chancel.

windows as at Cotton. The north clerestory is similar, but with emblems below the string course also, as at Bacton.

Simple, vertically-proportioned panelling that echoes the rhythms of the fenestration makes perhaps more fitting architectural decoration for a clerestory than individual emblems or chequerwork. This is demonstrated by the sense of tranquillity of the clerestory flushwork at Earl Stonham (plate 40) in comparison with the complication of the multiple themes in the elaborate, if spectacular, display at Woolpit (colour plate XIII).

CHANCELS, CHAPELS AND AISLES

Except on buttresses and plinths, only a few churches have flushwork on their chancels; on the east walls at Southwold, Mutford (plate 42), Mellis, Beeston St Lawrence (plate 53) and Beccles there are panelled dados with a band of quatrefoils above at Beccles. At Cromer, the chancel and aisles both have dado panelling, which is more ornate on the chancel east wall.

Considered by many to be amongst the foremost works in the medium, flushwork interpretations of the window tracery at the church of St Michael at Coslany, Norwich (plate 43) have been developed into an intricate panelling pattern entirely covering the south and east walls of the early sixteenth-century south aisle. An attribute that gives this work its special quality is the subtle variations in the widths of the stone elements of the primary frameworks of the panels, the tracery and the smaller details. The south and east chancel walls were refaced in the nineteenth century, reiterating the feigned window panelling theme used on the south aisle walls and maintaining the standard of quality.

The chancel east wall at Wiveton has a pair of two-stage foliated panels each side of the window and remnants of similar panelling on the south wall; Blythborough chancel also has panelling each side of the east window as well as the lettering below it mentioned in Chapter two. On the east end of the Victorian chancel at Wangford, a band of three large quatrefoils with small panels between seems oppressively dominant and out of scale with the window above.

plate 43. Superb flushwork wall panelling on the south aisle, St Michael at Coslany, Norwich.

Chequer flushwork covers the whole of the chancel east wall at Horsham St Faith and the date 1600 appears in flushwork in the gable peak; Hardingham chancel also has similar work on the east end above the level of the window-cill string course. The chancel at Martham has a fine chequer dado with beautifully squared flints and at Walberswick, varieties of small chequer form a narrow band of decoration on the rebuilt east wall of the south aisle which now serves as the nave and chancel of this evocative half-ruined church. Chequer is also conspicuous on the east gables and other Victorian parts of churches at Hadstock and St Mary Stoke, Ipswich, and on the modern east end of Chelmsford Cathedral. The fourteenth-century walls of the eastern bay of Lawford chancel are chequered with brick and knapped flint up to window-cill level (colour plate X).

At Long Melford, paired panels under combined canopy-heads, as used on the clerestory, are repeated as the main flushwork theme on the walls of the Lady Chapel which is entirely faced with flushwork, but indiscriminate unrelated motifs introduced into the three gables of the east wall are oddly incongruous relative to the rhythmic discipline of the panelling below (plate 73).

Although there is none on tower, clerestory or chancel, the flushwork of Glemsford church is its most memorable exterior feature.

The south aisle wall is entirely decorated with paired panels similar to those at Cavendish and Long Melford; these are continued along the side walls of the porch and so flushwork is continuous on the south elevation between tower and chancel.

A flushwork pattern that is quite different from any others is associated with an incredible window in the chancel east wall of Barsham church (frontispiece). It has to be seen to be believed! A lattice of stone strips overlays the whole wall area making a continuous pattern of diamonds that are infilled with knapped flint. The wall contains a large pointed east window and where the pattern meets the edges of the window the lines of the stone strips are continued across it as diagonal mullions so that the criss-cross pattern remains unbroken over the whole elevation. This extraordinary spectacle, probably of the sixteenth century and thought possibly to be a rebus of the shield of Sir Edward Etchingham, the church's patron in the sixteenth century, seems to have no historical derivation. The only other comparable pattern known to the author, the tower parapet of Althorne church (plate 34), seems an unlikely precedent if it is earlier.

plate 44. Decorative patterns on the diagonal buttresses of Dalham church tower

## Buttresses

As virtually all buttresses on Gothic flint churches have stone dressings on their corners, their outer faces readily lend themselves to the arranging of the knapped flintwork between the angle stones into flushwork patterns, and the buttresses on countless churches and their towers display square or rectangular chequers. Panels, singly or in pairs, are no less common and their vertical emphasis on a buttress visually augments its architectural role. A curious abnormality occurs on the diagonal buttresses of

Kessingland tower where, not at an offset but about halfway up the second stage, the flushwork abruptly converts from paired panels to an unusual staggered chequer scheme. Such a pronounced change of pattern may indicate the hand of a different master mason for the work from that level upwards, or alternatively, since the narrower buttresses in the tower's next stage would scarcely be wide enough to accommodate paired panels, the variation might simply be the start of a theme suitable for their reduced width. In either case it is strange that the change was not made at a tower stage level.

Many buttresses also provide the setting for emblems – Ixworth, Worlingworth and Stratford St Mary have notable examples as well as those at Elmswell, Northwold, Garboldisham and Badwell Ash mentioned earlier. By comparison with their medieval predecessors, the patterns made with geometric motifs on the wide buttresses of the seventeenth-century tower of Dalham church (plate 44) seem to be rather more simply decorative than symbolic.

plate 45. Stonework detail at the top of flushwork panels of porch buttresses at Pulham St Mary.

Buttresses with a greater than normal projection may have flushwork on their flanks. Those on the south side of Martham church and on the tower at St Peter's, Thetford, are impressive for the quality of their chequerwork, the flints of the former being beautifully squared (plate 57). Many porches also have panelling on the flanks of their buttresses and of those, a charming and probably unique panelling variation is found at Pulham St Mary where shallow-sunk foliated stone panel-heads have deeper-sunk spandrels, allowing crocketting in full relief and small sculptured faces within the spandrels (plate 45).

Polygonal buttresses are usually found only on major towers. Those on the similar towers at Redenhall, Eye and Laxfield and at St Mary's, Bungay, are generously patterned with flushwork panelling, and the great west tower of Wymondham Abbey has panels of proudwork on the upper stages of its polygonal buttresses. On a smaller scale, those on the porch at Woodbridge are decorated with emblems on their plinths and panelling above in the middle stages. Crowned with crocketted pinnacles, polygonal buttresses with flushwork panelling at the four corners of eighteenth-century Beeston Hall built in the Gothick style are reminiscent of those at the east corners of the Decorated chancel of Bradfield church in Norfolk.

Proudwork panels appear on buttresses at a few churches, the finest being those on the south aisle at St Margaret's church, Lowestoft, where the infilled knapped flints are squared. Tower buttresses at Great Massingham (plate 56) have paired proudwork panels, their knapped flints being white as also are those in the proudwork buttresses on the front of the porch at Wickmere.

SECULAR BUILDINGS

A date of circa 1320–25, established by the heraldry displayed on the north front, places Butley Priory Gatehouse as one of the earliest datable buildings with flushwork decoration. However, the curvilinear style of the flushwork decoration suggests a rather later date and because of successive eighteenth-century restorations, there is no certainty that all of what is seen today is original.

Rising between projecting bays, formerly the gatehouse towers but now truncated, the central gable of the north front accommodates two entrance arches – a wide carriage entry and a lower pedestrian one. Large pointed trefoils fill the spandrels over the former and a large cinquefoil surrounded by mouchettes occupies the space above the smaller arch; both are in flushwork. Above these arches, five rows of armorial bearings in relief stonework form a chequer pattern with squares of knapped flint, and above that a central window is flanked by flushwork feigned windows with curvilinear tracery. The projecting bays have a flushwork feigned window on the front, each with different curvilinear tracery, and a panel of chequer on their inner flank walls.

If the restoration of Burnham Norton Friary Gatehouse of the early fourteenth century is faithful to the original, its blank window replicas in proudwork on the west and east walls (plate 31) may represent the earliest use of that style as wall-surface decoration. The recessing behind the face of their stone dressings of the knapped flint infilling in the two single-light trefoiled blank windows on the west front can easily be recognised as a simple progression from the flush flint infilling of the blank lancets in the West Somerton belfry described earlier. Recessing of the flint infilling in blank windows of more than one light would leave their intermediate stonework in relief, proud of

**St Ethelbert's Gate, Norwich**

Top left
plate 46. West front prior to restoration.

Top right
plate 47. West front today.

Bottom left
plate 48. East front prior to restoration.

Bottom right
plate 49. East front today.

## The Architectural Setting    45

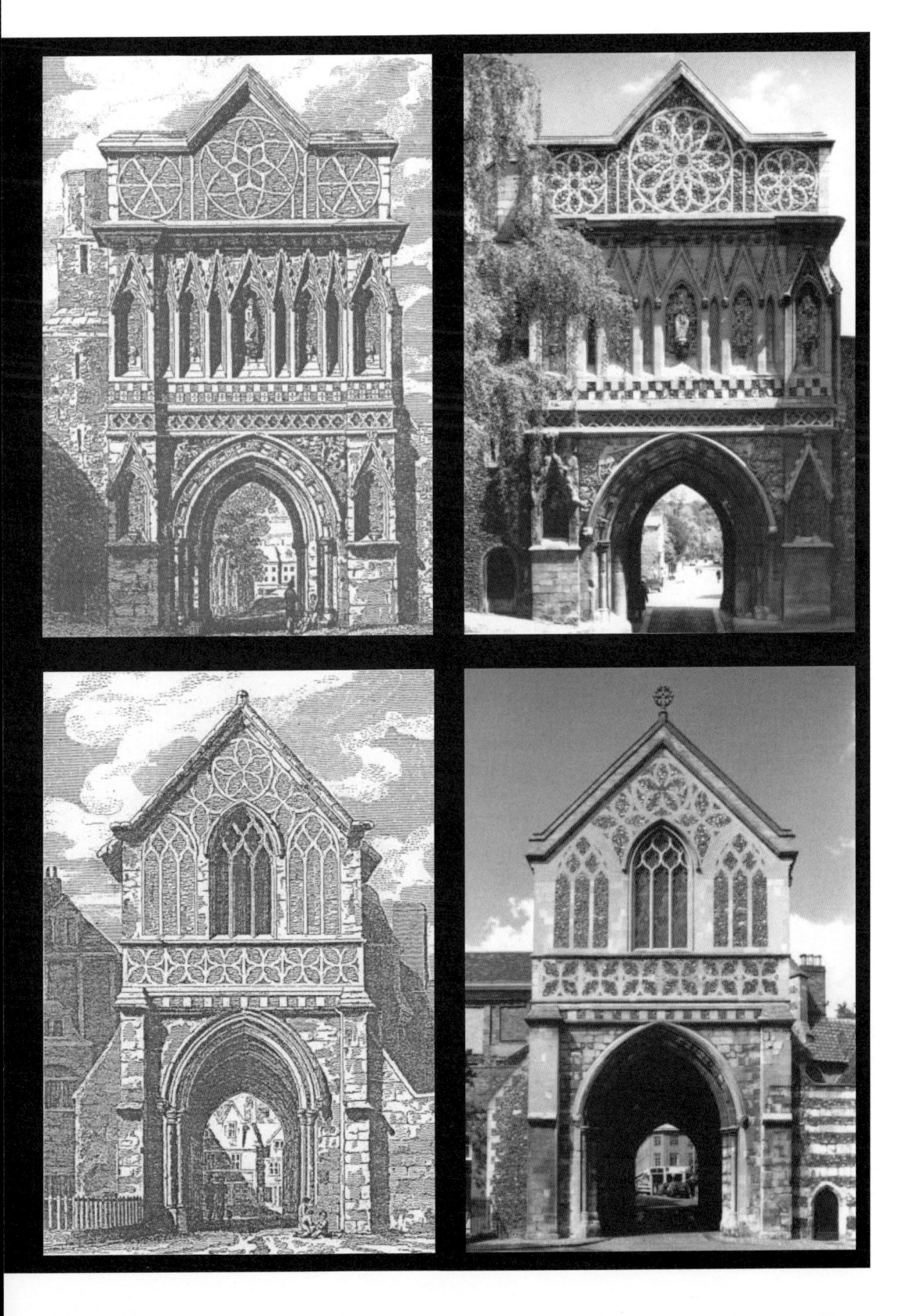

the infilling and conducive to receiving cusping and tracery detailing. This happens in the two-light blank windows on the west front that have Decorated tracery and the three-light ones on the east wall with cusped intersected tracery. These tracery patterns and other details of the building would accord with a date contemporary with Butley Priory Gatehouse.

The flushwork of St Ethelbert's Gate, Norwich, is notable for its circular 'rose window' motifs – three in the west parapet and one in

plate 50. Varied wall panelling and chequer parapets provide the splendid flushwork on the Gatehouse of St Osyth's Priory.

the gable of the east elevation. Although restored in the nineteenth century by William Wilkins, his flushwork design for the west parapet (plate 47) follows the general composition of what was there before as illustrated by R. Cattermole for Britton's *History and Antiquities of the See and Cathedral Church of Norwich* published in 1815 (plate 46), but the detail of the circular motifs is more elaborate. The flushwork design on the east side (plate 49) closely follows Cattermole's illustration of what preceded it (plate 48).

Although there are only a few secular buildings with flushwork, the quality of that on the Gatehouse of St Osyth's Priory, built in the late fifteenth century, matches in splendour any to be seen on churches. Rising from a two-stage flushwork plinth, divided by a string course into two main stages, and crowned with a battlemented parapet chequered with straight and diagonal squares, the south front (plate 50) is patterned with flushwork panelling in tiers whose heights are skilfully proportioned to relate to the architectural features of the façade. The lower stage has three tiers of panelling and the upper stage two, of which the topmost is almost three times taller than the others and its panels are paired to terminate with canopied and crocketted heads.

Also of the fifteenth century but much restored in the nineteenth, the Gatehouse of St John's Abbey in Colchester is comparable to St Osyth's in the luxuriance of its flushwork which covers the north façade facing the road. Panelling is the theme of the flushwork but it relates less harmoniously to the building's architectural features.

On a more domestic scale, the sixteenth-century Prior's Porch at Castle Acre Priory incorporates an area of very fine chequer flushwork above the entrance arch (colour plate XVII).

In addition to municipal displays of chequer flushwork on the Guildhalls in Norwich and King's Lynn (see page 13), brief mention should be made of two houses. St Peter's Hall, at South Elmham St Peter was built shortly after the dissolution of the monasteries in the sixteenth century, apparently incorporating re-cycled material from former church buildings: this included flushwork emblems, many of which were set in the plinth and porch on the north side of the house. At Shadwell Park, which is not accessible to the public, the nineteenth-century architect Teulon, who added the east entrance tower to the house, faced its upper stage and staircase turret with flushwork panelling.

Colour Plate I

Southwold church. The pattern on the side parapet of the porch is an interpretation in flushwork of the relief carving on the front parapet.

Colour Plate II

Great Witchingham church. Brick flushwork forming a diaper pattern in the clerestory walls with a stone flushwork feigned window at the west end.

Colour Plate III

Little Walsingham Priory ruins. Flushwork feigned windows on the corner turrets and the flanks of the buttresses.

Colour Plate IV

Hopton church. The belfry of the tower was rebuilt in the eighteenth century on the medieval lower stage in a simple classical style with chequer flushwork walls.

Colour Plate V

East Tuddenham. Crowned flushwork lettering in Lombardic script, reading GLORIATIBITR, on the front of the church porch.

Colour Plate VI

Ixworth Thorpe. Brick flushwork panelling in the side parapet and buttresses of the church porch.

Colour Plate VII

Papworth St Agnes church. All the walls of this nineteenth-century church and tower are arrestingly faced with a lapped chequer of unknapped flushwork.

Colour Plate VIII

Salcott church porch. The panels in the gable are infilled with knapped and rubble flints mixed with septaria.

Colour Plate IX

Kersey church tower. This parapet has more luxuriant flushwork than the majority of single-stage battlemented parapets.

Colour Plate X

Lawford church. Brick and flint chequer flushwork in the chancel walls.

Colour Plate XI

Redenhall church tower. With Eye and Laxton, one of the trio of splendid East Anglian towers with west fronts entirely faced wth flushwork panelling.

Colour Plate XII

St Lawrence's church, Ipswich. The two upper stages of this five-stage tower, with their striking flushwork and stonework, were rebuilt in 1882.

Colour Plate XIII

Chequer, emblems and panelling in spectacular flushwork on the clerestory of Woolpit church.

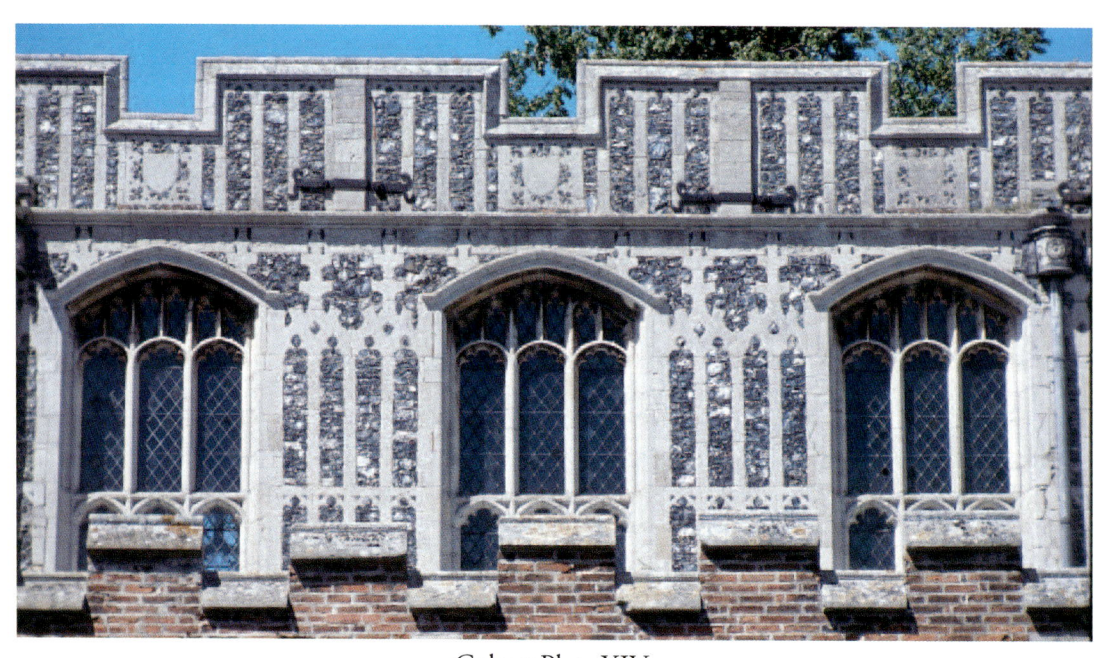

Colour Plate XIV

Cavendish church. Canopied paired flushwork panels in the clerestory and single panels in the parapet merlons with shield emblems between.

Colour Plate XV

Chelmsford Cathedral. A visual feast of flushwork themes in the side wall of the porch.

Colour Plate XVI

Great Barton church tower has a fine two-stage stepped parapet with flushwork panelling and emblems.

Colour Plate XVII

Castle Acre Priory, outer porch of the Prior's Lodgings. Chequer flushwork over entrance archway.

**Colour Plate XVIII**

Barton Bendish, St Andrew's. Inset flushwork on south porch incorporating the St Andrew's cross. The stone motifs in the gable are carved in shallow relief.

CHAPTER FIVE

# Kindred Features

It goes without saying that within a particular style of architecture, similar features constantly recur in countless different buildings, but where an idiosyncrasy, untypical of the normal vocabulary of the style, is found on more than one building there is reason to suppose that this is not just coincidence; it suggests that one of the instances was directly inspired by the other or perhaps the same mason was involved. This can apply to architectural design and decoration as well as to details of flushwork. Several such relationships between buildings have been noticed and usually they are found in buildings in the same locality but not always.

Reference has already been made to the church towers at Redenhall, Eye and Laxfield. Situated within about ten miles of each other, their architectural design is so similar as clearly to suggest a common inspiration. All three towers have four stages, polygonal buttresses, a west doorway surmounted by a large four-light window whose arch penetrates the second stage, and virtually identical two-light windows in the second and third stages of the west front. The flushwork too is similar: alternating bands of wide and narrow panelling entirely cover the west fronts with small areas of chequer introduced above or below the second- and third-stage windows and corresponding flushwork on the top stages only of the other elevations, except that there is none on the south face at Redenhall.

There is also an obvious likeness between the design and flushwork of the eight-pinnacled stepped parapets on the church towers at Helmingham (dated 1543) and Horham about ten miles away; likewise, battlemented parapets on the neighbouring towers at Yoxford and Kelsale both have unusual and intricate flushwork comprising two-stage panelling in the merlons and elaborated quatrefoils flanked by single panels below the indents.

plate 51. Flushwork on the tower west wall at Coltishall.

Having in mind the comparative rarity of proudwork, it seems more than a coincidence that the churches at Shipdham, Mattishall and North Tuddenham (plate 32), within a compass of seven miles, all have tower parapet designs of similar, but not identical proudwork. North Creake, North Elmham and Castle Acre, all in north-west Norfolk, have already been mentioned as having proudwork tower parapets of the type with the flatter stone elements, and of the occasional octagonal belfries on circular towers that have proudwork feigned windows, those at Quidenham and Poringland (plate 59) are noteable for their identical tracery pattern.

Although other churches whose tower parapets have 'Norwich' style flushwork are quite widely spread in north-east Norfolk (see Appendix D), the concentration within Norwich of four such towers suggests that this was a local style originating in the city from where it reached a few outlying places. These distant towers are probably later than the Norwich ones that date from the mid-fifteenth century.

On the churches of Long Melford and Cavendish, less than four miles apart, the only significant differences in the design of their clerestories arise from the closer spacing of the windows at Long Melford and the additional height above them for an inscription. The parapet designs, the flushwork theme and the windows themselves, of uncommon three-light pattern with intermediate transomes and depressed two-centred arches, are all virtually identical. A known link here is the Smyth family that was associated with the fifteenth-century work at both churches.

The porches of the neighbouring churches of Hitcham (plate 38), Felsham and Preston show obvious similarities. All are single-storey parapetted designs with angle buttresses; their frontal flushwork is similar and the front buttresses on each have stone panels in their lower stages and a niche in the upper. At Hitcham and Felsham though, there is no side-wall flushwork as at Preston except on plinth and parapet.

Another group of porches at Halesworth (plate 24), Huntingfield and Blyford, again near neighbours, also demonstrates a close affinity. They are architecturally similar, having diagonal buttresses and low-pitched uncrenellated front parapets decorated with wavy tracery in relief stonework; the arrangement of the flushwork is the same on all and although the detail differs a little, a rare touch common to all is the placing of small quatrefoils or foliated shields below the panels of a series. This, with the other likenesses, seems to be a definite signature unifying the three works. By contrast with these assured designs, rather spare flushwork links the almost identical porches at Moulton St Michael and Aslacton, where the chief feature of their similar flushwork is a single foliated panel each side of the entrance. These two churches are less than a mile apart.

At Coltishall, north of Norwich, a recurring motif is the crowned initial I (for John); it appears in the tower parapet and plinth and in a band of flushwork emblems over the west door alternating with a circular emblem containing a blank shield surrounded by lobes (plate 51). This is an unusual combination and so it comes as a surprise to find the same grouping of motifs on the south aisle parapet of the church dedicated to St Matthew, in Ipswich. The south aisle is said to have been widened in 1845 and refaced in 1884.[1]

A flushwork base course on Thrandeston church tower consists of repeated emblems of an unusual design (plate 52) that has wavy strips in the upper corners of each rectangular element and a central pointed quatrefoil on which is superimposed a smaller stone and flint motif.

plate 52. Repetitive emblems on the base of Thrandeston tower.

Some distance away at Theberton comparative symbols, though without the superimposed motif, are used in a continuous repetitive band on the base and buttresses of the church porch in the same way as on the Thrandeston tower. The device and its similar application on the two buildings seem to indicate a connection.

Finally, an oddity. A curious departure from normal practice is seen in the church tower parapet at Benacre and also at Sibton, about fourteen miles away. The parapets are built of cobble flints, and three isolated flushwork features consisting of simple tracery-based knapped flint motifs framed in stone are inset within the cobbles; they appear to be unrelated to the architecture and give the impression of being afterthoughts. It is as if they had been re-assembled from salvaged stonework and reset within rebuilt flintwork. These seem to be the only examples of isolated flushwork elements set within a background of cobble flints.

---

1  N. Pevsner. (revised E. Radcliffe) *The Buildings of England. Suffolk*. Penguin 1974.

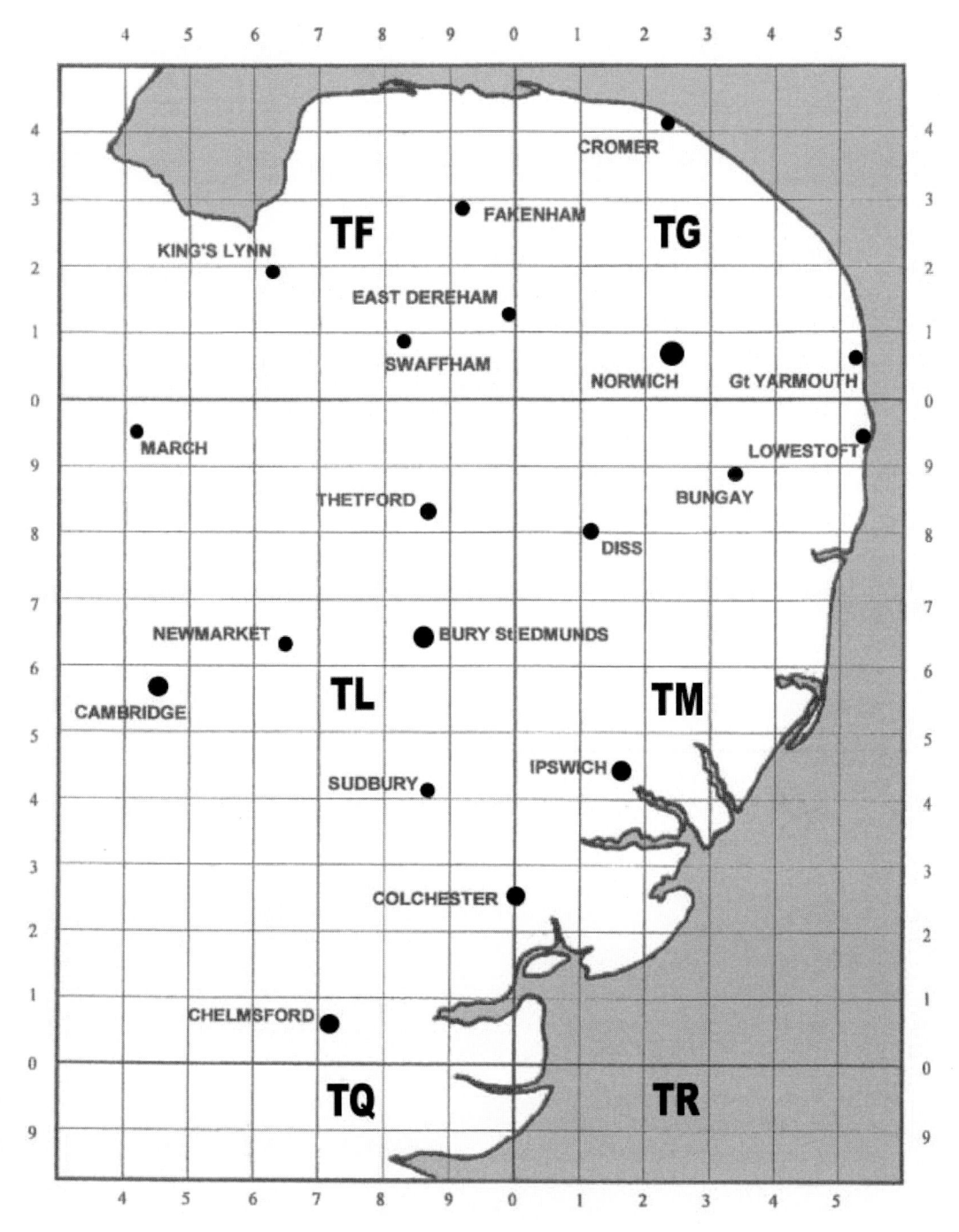

Fig 3  Map of East Anglia
Scale: 1 cm = 10 km

The numbers denoting the grid lines that define the left side and lower edges respectively of the ten-kilometre squares shown on this map correspond with the first and fourth digits of the six-figure map references of places in the Gazetteer. These squares, together with the reference letters of the larger National Grid squares, establish the whereabouts of those places.

# The Gazetteer

This directory describes briefly the flushwork of the majority of buildings in East Anglia on which it occurs, but no claim is made that every single building with any flushwork on it is represented. Several churches, for instance, may have a little flushwork on their buttresses only, and some such as these may not have been included. All entries refer to the churches of the places named unless otherwise stated.

Almost all the churches mentioned are built of flint – as-found, knapped or mixed – or of flint interspersed with erratics, ferricrete, bricks or stone; where otherwise, the materials are stated.

Chequerwork of flint and stone is a theme that, as mentioned earlier, also occurs in flint areas other than East Anglia, for example in parts of Wiltshire, Dorset and Sussex, but in those parts it is not known as flushwork; the following gazetteer therefore does not include instances of flint and stone chequer-patterned walls outside the East Anglian region.

Tower parapet types are described by the abbreviations used in the diagram on page 30, i.e. 1B and 1S for single-stage battlemented and stepped types, and 2B and 2S for the two-stage battlemented and stepped equivalents. Porches are single-storey unless otherwise stated.

As in the preceding text, figures in parentheses are the reference numbers of the plates, those in Roman numerals refer to the coloured plates.

Entries marked with an asterisk indicate works that are considered as being of particular interest by virtue of the quality of their flushwork or because of unusual or distinctive features.

# NORFOLK

### ACLE                  TG 401103

Tower:     Round tower with octagonal upper stage. Panelling on 1B parapet.
North Porch:     Panelling on front up to arch-springing level.

### ALBURGH                  TM 271873

Tower:*     1S parapet with panelling and emblems. Emblems include wheel motif. Panelled base. Group of four panels each side of tower west door.

### ALDBOROUGH                  TG 179338

South Porch:     Proudwork panelling on buttresses.

### ALDEBY                  TM 450934

Tower:     1S parapet with panelling. Thick stonework between panels looks restored.
North Porch:     Panelling on front and buttresses and on base of side walls.

### ASHWELLTHORPE                  TM 147977

Tower:     1B parapet with buff brick chequer flushwork squares of one-brick size seen more clearly on E and N than S and W. Smaller stone chequer and panels on wide diagonal buttresses.
South Porch:     Two-storey. One stage of separate single panels at arch level.
Nave:     Single-course chequer plinth on south side.
North Chapel:     Ditto on west wall.

### ASLACTON                  TM 156911

South Porch:     Large single panel on each side of entrance with two panels above. Similar to nearby Moulton but slightly different detail.

### ATTLEBOROUGH                  TM 049954

Nave, Transepts:     One course rectangular chequer on plinths. Feigned window above south door.

## AYLMERTON  TG 183401

Tower: Round tower with circular 1B parapet with panelling.

## AYLSHAM  TG 193270

Tower: 1B parapet with panelling.
South Porch: Two-storey, with panelling on front.

## BANNINGHAM  TG 215295

Tower: 1B parapet has panelling with white knapped flint. Base and buttresses have proudwork panelling.

## BARNHAM BROOM  TG 082078

Tower: 1B parapet with panelling and emblems.

## BARTON BENDISH, St Andrew's (XVIII)  TF 713057

South Porch:* Blank shields and saltire crosses inset in front wall and buttresses, and shallow relief stone panels inset in gable. Band of blank shields with knapped flint between below window in side walls.

## BARTON TURF  TG 343219

Tower: 1B parapet with panelling and quatrefoils, the flintwork slightly recessed but stone elements flat, unlike in true proudwork. Base of two stages alternating stone and knapped flint squares.
North Porch: Two-storey. Panelling on front only. Where they meet, the foliated heads of paired panels in each of the parapet merlons rest improbably on small blank shields in place of the normal central mullion. cf. Postwick tower. Panelled base.

## BEACHAMWELL (37)  TF 751054

Tower:* Round tower with octagonal upper stage. Feigned two-light windows in diagonals above which on SE and SW faces mosaic-like motifs in different-coloured knapped flints.

## BEDINGHAM  TM 285934

Tower: Round tower with octagonal upper stage. Feigned two-light windows in diagonal faces.

**BEESTON**                                                                    TF 894153

North Porch:     Chequer on front. Panelling on buttresses.

**BEESTON HALL**                                 TG 332215

Corners of
  house:       Panelling on polygonal buttresses.

**BEESTON REGIS**                             TG 173432

Tower:           Level parapet of two shallow stages with simple panelling in lower stage, of white flints.

**BEESTON ST LAWRENCE (53)**             TG 328220

South Porch:     Panelled base.
Chancel:*        Dado of wide blank arcading on east end.

**BEIGHTON**                                               TG 386083

Tower:           1B parapet with panelling in merlons. Relief stonework below indents looks recently restored.

**BELAUGH**                                                  TG 288185

Tower:           Single-stage level parapet with uniform panelling.

plate 53. Beeston St Lawrence. Dado on chancel east end.

### BERGH APTON    TM 311999

Tower: 1B parapet with brick chequer flushwork. Chequer squares are one-and-a-half-brick size.

### BILLINGFORD (near Dereham)    TG 013205

Tower: Octagonal. 1B parapet, panelled.

### BLAKENEY    TG 033436

Tower: Proudwork base and buttresses. Two-course chequer band over west door.
S E Stair Turret: Panelled base.
South Aisle: Panelled base on west wall. Single panels on both stages of buttresses.
North Aisle: West wall base panelled. Proudwork panels on buttresses.

### BLICKLING    TG 178285

South Porch: Panelling on gable.
South Aisle: Panels on buttress plinths.
North Aisle: Simple alternating stone and knapped flint squares on buttress plinths.

plate 54. Breckles. Chequer patterning on the octagonal belfry.

## BLOFIELD  TG 335093

Tower: 'Norwich' style 1B parapet with relief stone motifs inset. Panelled base and buttresses.

## BRADFIELD  TG 268334

Chancel:* Polygonal NE and SE pinnacled buttresses have panelled faces.

## BRANCASTER  TF 772439

Tower: 1B parapet with panelling. Vertical chequer on buttresses.

## BRANDON PARVA  TG 070081

Tower: 1B parapet with panelling and emblems.

## BRECKLES (54)  TL 958946

Tower: Round tower with octagonal belfry stage with chequer on diagonal faces.

## BRESSINGHAM  TM 077808

Tower: 1B parapet with panelling. Panelled base and buttresses. Two courses of chequer between west doorway and window above.

Clerestory:* Two-stage. Lower stage elegant panelling; upper stage stone arch voussoirs alternating with knapped flint.

## BRETTENHAM  TL 932834

Tower: 1B parapet with panelling.

## BRIDGHAM  TL 957858

North Porch: Remnants of panelling once covering front and sides, much now lost through ruthless repairs.

## BRISLEY  TF 950215

Tower: Panelled base. Proudwork panelled buttresses.

## BROCKDISH  TM 204796

Tower: 1B parapet with chequer. Chequer on buttresses.

| | |
|---|---|
| South Porch: | Panelling on front and buttresses. Also chequer cross on buttresses. |
| South Aisle: | Panelling on parapet and vertical chequer on buttresses. |

## BROOME  TM 347933

Tower: Panelled base. 1B parapet with shallow-sunk stone head panelling.

## BRUNSTEAD  TG 370268

Tower: Simple square panels in plinth.

## BUNWELL  TM 125928

Tower: 1B parapet with panelling and emblems. Panelled buttresses with crowned M emblem.

South Porch:* Gabled front. Front and side walls panelled. The flushwork is galleted.

## BURGH NEXT AYLSHAM  TG 218251

Tower: 1B parapet with 'Norwich' style panelling. Relief crowned Ms in outer merlons and relief lozenges in centre merlons; flush blank shields in indents. Small blank shields round all the motifs. Panelled base.

## BURGH ST MARGARET (Fleggburgh)  TG 444140

Tower: 'Norwich' style 1B parapet with flush crowned Ms in the three centre zones.

## BURGH ST PETER  TM 493937

Tower: Base stage has brick diaper pattern within knapped flint.

## BURLINGHAM St Andrew  TG 365101

Tower: Panelled base, continued on diagonal buttresses. On north side, plain rectangular panels with wide stone verticals between, with shallow relief carving. 'Norwich' style 1B parapet.

## BURNHAM NORTON, Friary Gatehouse (31)  TF 838428

East Front:* Cusped intersected tracery blank windows in proudwork

| | |
|---|---|
| West Front:* | flanking central proudwork niche above entrance archway.<br>One-light proudwork feigned windows each side of recessed entry. Two-light traceried proudwork feigned windows flanking central window at upper level. |

## BURNHAM THORPE                                              TF 852418

| | |
|---|---|
| Chancel:* | East end: Dado of rectangular chequer in dark flint. Below the window, six proudwork panels. Each side of lower part of window, a random chequer in dark flint. In the gable, a chequer of white flint. |

## BYLAUGH                                                       TG 036184

| | |
|---|---|
| Tower: | Round, with octagonal upper stage. Proudwork two-light feigned windows in diagonals, replicating belfry openings. |

## CAISTOR ST EDMUND                                        TG 233034

| | |
|---|---|
| Tower: | 1B parapet with simple panelling in brick flushwork. |

## CARBROOKE                                                    TF 949022

| | |
|---|---|
| Tower: | Panelled base. |
| North Porch: | Two-storey. Panelled front. Panelled base on side walls. |
| Aisles: | Panelled bases. |

## CARLETON RODE                                              TM 115925

| | |
|---|---|
| Tower: | Single course of horizontal chequer on base. One course chequer below parapet. On east face of tower, south of nave ridge, tall plain rectangular panels extend from nave roof to tower parapet. |
| South Aisle: | Large rectangular panels in two stages on west end wall. |

## CASTLE ACRE                                                   TF 816148

| | |
|---|---|
| Tower: | 1B parapet with proudwork panelling with chamfered-edge stonework. |

## CASTLE ACRE PRIORY, Prior's Lodging (XVII)      TF 814147

| | |
|---|---|
| Outer Porch: | Broad band of chequer over entrance. |

## CLEY NEXT THE SEA            TG 049432

| | |
|---|---|
| South Porch: | Two-storey. Openwork parapet above frieze of small proudwork quatrefoils. |
| Stair Turret: | As porch. |
| South Aisle: | Panelled parapet with white flint. |
| North Clerestory: | Two-stage parapet, upper stage proudwork with panels in merlons and quatrefoils and panels below indents, lower stage a single course of chequer squares. |

## COLBY            TG 220313

South Porch: Two-storey. Panelled base except the repaired stretches on side walls. On the front, two tall finialled panels each side of entrance arch. Above the arch, a band of panelling with shallow-relief stone shields below alternate panels; the centre panel has small shields each side of its finial head.

## COLTISHALL (51)            TG 272198

| | |
|---|---|
| Tower: | 'Norwich' style 1B parapet with inset crowned initials I and small blank shields. Emblems in base. Four panels each side of west door and band of emblems above, comprising alternating crowned initials I and blank shield in circle. |
| North Porch: | Panelled base on front and sides. |

## COLTON            TG 104093

Tower: 1B parapet with panelling.

## COSTESSEY            TG 177126

South Porch: Diagonal chequer in base of front and side walls. Panelling on front up to gable level and on sides up to window-head level, with remnants above.

## CRIMPLESHAM            TF 655038

Tower: Carstone flushwork on buttresses.

## CROMER (front cover)            TG 220424

| | |
|---|---|
| Tower: | Inset emblems in wall of top stage. |
| South Porch: | Two-storey. Two-stage panelling up to arch springing level on front and sides. |
| North Porch: | As South Porch. |

| | |
|---|---|
| Aisles:* | Panelled dado with blank shields in spandrels above a stone relief base. Buttresses have flushwork panel on lower stage, proudwork panel on middle stage and stone niche in upper. |
| Chancel:* | Panelled dado as aisles, but below the east window the dado panels are taller and incorporate intermediate crocketted finial motifs. |
| Clerestory: | Feigned two-light window at west end, both sides. |

## CROXTON (near Thetford)      TL 874867

| | |
|---|---|
| Chancel: | Proudwork on NE buttress. |

## DEOPHAM (55)      TG 050005

| | |
|---|---|
| Tower:* | Angle buttresses with vertical chequer pattern support polygonal corner turrets at top of tower. Two-stage panelling on turret faces with panels and quatrefoils in turret battlements. 1B parapets with panelling and emblems are interrupted by central triangular gables containing feigned rose window motif. |

## DICKLEBURGH (30)      TM 168825

| | |
|---|---|
| Tower: | 1B parapet. In each merlon, a single foliated panel infilled with cobbles; between these, below each indent, nine squares of chequer. |

plate 55. Deopham. Rose window motif in tower parapet.

South Porch: Panelling on front. Panelled base and parapet on side walls. Small cross motif in diagonal chequer in stone face of buttresses.

## DILHAM                                                                                                    TG 326259

Chancel: Built 1931. Three flushwork panels below east window.

## DISS                                                        TM 118801

South Porch: Diagonal chequer base on front and side walls. One stage of panels with emblems above on front and buttresses. Panelling on low-pitch gable.
South Aisle: Panelled buttresses.
Chancel: Panelled buttresses with emblems on plinths. Modern.

## DITCHINGHAM                            TM 330923

Tower: 'Norwich' style partly battlemented parapet (reduced centre merlon) with inset relief stone lozenges.
South Porch: Panelled base on front.

## EAST DEREHAM                         TF 986134

South Porch: Two-storey. Two narrow rectangular panels each side of entrance arch, with shallow relief stone heads. Single emblem below, each side. Panelling on diagonal buttresses.

## EAST HARLING                        TL 990868

South Porch: Panelled front and east wall.

## EAST RAYNHAM                     TF 880225

Tower: 1B parapet with panelling.
South Porch: Panelling in gable.

## EAST TUDDENHAM (V)                TG 085115

South Porch:* Inscription over entrance in crowned Lombardic script: GLORIATIBITR. In gable, a single-light proudwork feigned window each side of central niche. Panelled base on front and side walls and buttresses.

## EATON                                     TG 202059

Tower: 1B parapet with panelling and emblems. Large quatrefoil on north wall.

## EDGEFIELD            TG 094343

| | |
|---|---|
| Aisles: | Two courses of chequer in a band at window shoulder level for full length and across west walls. |
| Nave: | Two similar chequer bands across west wall at same level and at window arch springing level. |
| Clerestory: | Similar chequer band halfway up on both sides. |
| Chancel: | On south wall, two similar chequer bands, one continuing the clerestory band, the other lower. Single band above east window. |

## ELLINGHAM            TM 366919

| | |
|---|---|
| Tower: | 1S parapet with panelling in merlons and steps, with shallow-sunk stone heads. |

## ELSING            TG 052167

| | |
|---|---|
| Tower: | 1B parapet with panelling and emblems. |

## ERPINGHAM            TG 198314

| | |
|---|---|
| Tower: | 1B 'Norwich' style parapet with inset carved stone lozenge emblems in each zone and four small shields in corners of merlon zones. |

## FAKENHAM            TF 919297

| | |
|---|---|
| Tower: | Panelled base. Two panels surmounted by an emblem each side of window on west. Proudwork buttresses. |

## FELBRIGG            TG 198390

| | |
|---|---|
| Tower: | Panelling on base. |
| North Porch: | Panels on front and on face of buttresses. |
| Nave: | Panelling on some buttresses. |

## FELMINGHAM            TG 252294

| | |
|---|---|
| Tower: | Panelled base. Three panels each side of west door. |

## FELTWELL, St Nicholas'            TL 713908

| | |
|---|---|
| Clerestory: | Emblems inset in the wall flintwork, two between each of the three windows and one each end were presumably originally flushwork but their stonework is now infilled with cement rendering. |

## FILBY  TG 469133

Tower: Panelled base. 1S parapet with thirteen zones. Emblems in indents and panels in merlons and steppings, some with shallow-sunk stone heads.

## FINCHAM  TF 688065

Tower: 1B parapet with panelling. At high level on each buttress, five emblems.
South Aisle: Battlemented parapet with panelled merlons and emblems in indents.
Chancel: Battlemented parapet with panelled merlons and emblems in indents.

## FORNCETT ST MARY  TM 166939

Tower: 1B parapet with panelling in west side only.

## FORNCETT ST PETER  TM 165928

North Porch: One stage of panels on front and diagonal buttresses. Emblem above arch.

## FOULSHAM  TG 033251

Tower: Panelling on base and buttresses and at sides of west door.

## FOXLEY  TG 039218

Tower: 1B parapet, panelled. Panel heads are stone with shallow-sunk foliations and the flint infill of the rectangular panels beneath is recessed to the same depth as the stonework sinkings.

## GARBOLDISHAM  TM 004816

Tower:* 1B parapet with panelling and emblems. Emblems on base and buttresses.
North Porch: Inscriptions on base and gable probably originally flushwork but all flint missing.

## GARVESTON  TG 023073

Tower: 1B parapet with panelling.

84  Flint Flushwork

## GAYTON                                              TF 730193

Tower:          1B parapet with panelling in poor condition.

## GIMINGHAM                                          TG 286367

South Porch:    Two-storey. Band of emblems on front, most flint missing. Small chequer in front parapet and emblems in side parapet.

plate 56. Great Massingham. Proudwork buttress on tower.

## GISSING                                      TM 146 853

North Porch:*   Two-storey. Panelling on front and buttresses. Panelled parapet on side walls.

## GORLESTON                                    TG 525044

Tower:          1B parapet, panelled.
South Porch:    Diagonal chequer over whole front.

## GREAT BIRCHAM                                TF 770327

North Porch:    Pair of panels each side of arch.

## GREAT CRESSINGHAM (12)                       TF 825018

South Porch:    Crowned sword and crowned M emblems in base, cf. Hilborough.

## GREAT DUNHAM                                 TF 873148

Tower:          1B parapet with cinquefoil panelling on west side only.

## GREAT ELLINGHAM                              TM 021971

Tower:          1B parapet with chequer. Two-course chequer base to west front and buttresses.
North Porch:    Chequer in gable but the squares in the gable peak are brick in lieu of stone.

## GREAT MASSINGHAM (56)                        TF 798230

Tower:          1B parapet with panelling. Panelled base and proudwork panelling on buttresses.
South Aisle:    Battlemented parapet with panelling in merlons and a chequer of four squares below indents. Buttresses chequer.

## GREAT MELTON                                 TG 141062

Tower:          1B parapet with panelling.

## GREAT PLUMSTEAD                              TM 301099

Tower:          C.18 brick tower with stone/flint chequer in parapet, but brick/flint of one-brick size on north face.

## GREAT WALSINGHAM                            TF 938377

   South Porch:     Chequer parapet on front and sides.
   North Vestry:    Identical flushwork to south porch.

## GREAT WITCHINGHAM (II)                      TG 103200

   Tower:            Panelling on base.
   South Porch:*    Canopied crowned monograms in panels on front of base and buttresses. Panels on base of side walls. Band of crowned monograms above 4-inch chequer course over arch.
   Clerestory:*     Feigned window at west end. Flush diaper pattern of red brick within knapped flint between clerestory windows.

## GREAT YARMOUTH, St Mary's R.C.              TG 529077

   Tower:            Panels each side of north door. 1S parapet with inset emblems in centre merlon, other zones panelled. Panelled buttresses. Upper stages of SW stair turret panelled. Chequer plinth,
   North Aisle:     Panelled buttresses.
   Chancel:         Panelled diagonal butresses.

## GREAT YARMOUTH, St Nicholas'                TG 524080

   South Porch:     Band of chequer above entrance arch.

## GREAT YARMOUTH, St Spiridon                 TG 527071
### Greek Orthodox church, formerly St Peter's

   Tower:            Yellow brick. 1B parapet with rectangular panels.

## GREAT YARMOUTH,                             TG 524074
### former Congregational Church

   Aisle Turrets:    Chequer in peaks of small front and side gables of aisles' west turrets.

## GRISTON (6)                                 TL 943093

   Tower:*          'Norwich' style 1B parapet with inset emblems of crossed swords and crossed keys with blank shields. Emblems in base but much flint missing.

## GUNTHORPE                                   TG 013353

   Tower:*          1B parapet, chequer with quatrefoils in merlons. The knapped flint all white. Single course of chequer in base and vertical chequer on buttresses.

## HACKFORD         TG 059023

  South Porch:    Panelling in base and buttresses. Also proudwork on buttresses.

## HALES         TM 383961

  Tower:    Round tower with level circular parapet: chequer, but much of the stonework repaired with brick.

## HALVERGATE         TM 417067

  Tower:    Panelled base.

## HAPPISBURGH         TG 380312

  Tower:    1B parapet with panelling. Proudwork panelled base.
  South Porch:    Two-storey. Panelled parapets on front and side walls.
  Clerestory:    Panelled parapet.
  South Aisle:    Panelled parapet.

## HARDINGHAM         TG 035052

  Chancel:*    Whole of east end above cill-level string course chequer.

## HARDWICK         TM 223901

  South Porch:    Flint/brick chequer on front. The squares are half-brick size and the flint squares single flints.

## HASSINGHAM         TG 369055

  Tower:    Round tower with octagonal upper stage. Panelling in 1B parapet.

## HAVERINGLAND         TG 151209

  Tower:    Round tower with 1B parapet with simple uncusped arch motifs. The knapped flint infill is slightly recessed behind the faces of the stone members.

## HEDENHAM         TM 312934

  Tower:    1S parapet, panelled with emblems below indents.
  South Porch:    Feigned Perpendicular window in west wall.

## HEIGHAM · TG 213093

Tower: Tower only standing. 1B parapet with panelling.

## HEMSBY · TG 495175

Tower: 1B parapet with panelling and emblems. Panelled base.

## HETHERSETT · TG 161049

Tower: Chequer base and chequer on buttresses.

## HEVINGHAM · TG 201224

Tower: Single-stage level parapet with foliations.
Nave: Panelled parapet with date 1894 in flushwork.

## HICKLING · TG 414243

Tower: Single-course chequer base. 1B parapet with shallow proudwork panels in merlons and quatrefoils below indents.
South Porch: Two-storey. Level battlemented parapet with panels in merlons and quatrefoils below indents.

## HILBOROUGH · TF 825000

Tower: Pair of panels each side of west door.
South Porch: Crowned M and crowned sword emblems in base, cf. Great Cressingham.

## HOCKERING · TG 072133

Tower: 1B parapet with panelling and emblems. Chequer on buttresses.

## HONING · TG 325280

Tower: Panelled base. 1B parapet with panelling and emblems below indents. White flint.

## HONINGHAM · TG 115113

Tower: Deep 1B parapet. Panelling in two stages with castellated heads to lower panels.

## HORNING　　　　　　　　　　　　　　　　　TG 355166
Tower:　　　Large chequer base, then one course of small horizontal chequer above a stone moulding.

## HORSFORD　　　　　　　　　　　　　　　　TG 196154
Tower:　　　1B parapet with panelling and emblems.

## HORSHAM ST FAITH　　　　　　　　　　　　TG 215152
Tower:　　　1B parapet of knapped flint with inset stone blank shields in merlons.
Chancel:*　　Entire east wall chequer with flushwork; date 1600 in gable.

## HUNWORTH　　　　　　　　　　　　　　　TG 064356
Tower:　　　1B parapet with panelling in merlons and quatrefoils below indents. Vertical chequer on buttresses.
South Porch:　Emblems in plinth on front and buttresses.

## ICKBURGH　　　　　　　　　　　　　　　　TF 816950
Tower:　　　1B parapet with chequer on north and west faces only.

## ILLINGTON　　　　　　　　　　　　　　　　TF 948900
Tower:　　　1S parapet with diagonal chequer. Panelled base.

## INGHAM　　　　　　　　　　　　　　　　　TG 390260
Tower:　　　1S parapet with panelling. Panelled base and buttresses. Two panels each side of west door.

## KELLING　　　　　　　　　　　　　　　　　TG 089419
Tower:　　　1B parapet with diagonal chequer of white flint. Vertical chequer on buttresses.

## KENNINGHALL　　　　　　　　　　　　　　TM 041860
Tower:　　　Emblems on base and buttresses, but flint missing.
Nave:　　　Emblems on buttresses but flint also missing.

## KETTLESTONE　　　　　　　　　　　　　　TF 967318
Tower:　　　Octagonal, with single-stage level parapet, panelled.

90  *Flint Flushwork*

plate 57. Beautifully squared knapped flints on the flanks of the chancel buttresses at Martham.

**KING'S LYNN, All Saints**　　　　　　　　　　　　TF 621197

   Clerestories:    Slightly irregular chequer. Level parapet of knapped flint with Greek crosses of stone at intervals.
   Nave:    Gable parapets similar to clerestory parapets.

**KING'S LYNN, Guildhall**　　　　　　　　　　　　TF 617198

   Façades:*    Chequer.

## LANGHAM  TG 008412

    Tower:           Panelling on base and buttresses.
    Chancel:         Panelling on base of east bay.

## LARLING  TL 983897

    Tower:           Emblems on SW buttress and pair of panels on NW buttress.

## LIMPENHOE  TM 395040

    Tower:           Panelled base.

## LITTLE CRESSINGHAM  TF 872001

    Nave:            Three-light feigned window in west wall.

## LITTLE MASSINGHAM  TF 793242

    Tower:           Diaper pattern brick flushwork on stair turret.
    South Porch:    Two separate panels each side of arch, one on front, one on buttress splay.

## LITTLE WALSINGHAM, Priory Church Ruins (III)  TF 935365

    Chancel:*      Panelling on buttresses and wall of standing remnant of east end. Feigned windows under relief crocketted stone canopies in the lower stages.

## LODDON  TM 364988

    Tower:           1B parapet with panelling and emblems. Panelled base.
    South Porch:    Two-storey. Panelled front. Panelled base on side walls. Battlemented parapet with panelling and emblems on front and sides.

## LUDHAM  TG 388183

    North Porch:    Panelling on front and buttresses.

## MARTHAM (57)  TG 455185

    Tower:           1B parapet with panelling and emblems. Panelled base.
    South Porch:    Two-storey. Panelled base on front and side walls. A panel on each side of arch and on each side of upper window.

| | |
|---|---|
| South Aisle: | Panelled base and dado of blank shields. |
| Chancel:* | Panelled base and deep chequer dado, including on buttresses. |

## MATTISHALL                                                             TG 053110

| | |
|---|---|
| Tower: | 1B parapet with proudwork panelling and quatrefoils, cf. North Tuddenham and Shipdham. |
| South Porch: | Shallow-sunk stone-head panels on front. Vertical stonework elements of gable panels have relief mini-tabernacle decoration. |
| North Porch: | Panelling on base and parapets of front and side walls. |

## MILEHAM                                                                 TF 922197

| | |
|---|---|
| Tower: | 1B parapet with panelling. |

## MOULTON ST MICHAEL                      TM 166908

| | |
|---|---|
| South Porch: | Single panel each side of entrance, with two panels above in arch stage, cf. Aslacton. |

## MUNDHAM                                                   TM 325980

| | |
|---|---|
| Tower: | 1B parapet with panelling. |

## NARBOROUGH                                          TF 747130

| | |
|---|---|
| Tower: | 1B parapet with panelling. Panels have unusual shallow inverted-V heads. |

## NECTON                                                                TF 878098

| | |
|---|---|
| Tower: | Chequer base. |
| South Vestry: | Chequer base. |

## NEW BUCKENHAM                                 TM 088906

| | |
|---|---|
| Tower: | 1B parapet with brick chequer; chequer squares are one-and-a-half-brick size. Emblems in base but much flint missing. Panelling and emblems in buttresses. |
| South Porch: | One small stage of panelling on front. Panelling on parapets of front and side walls. |
| Clerestory: | Panelling below window shoulder height, with alternating brick and flint arch voussoirs above. |

## NORTH CREAKE                                     TF 854378

| | |
|---|---|
| Tower: | 1B parapet. Proudwork panelling with chamfered-edge stone elements. |

plate 58. Norwich, St Clement's. 'Norwich' style flushwork on the tower parapet.

## NORTH ELMHAM     TF 988217

Tower: 1B parapet with proudwork panelling. Knapped flint infilling to three-light blank windows in third stage.
South Porch: Single course of chequer on base.

## NORTH LOPHAM     TM 036826

Tower: Panels and emblems in base and buttresses. Shallow relief inscription stones inset in middle stage of south wall.
South Porch: A few squares of chequer in parapet.

## NORTHREPPS     TG 244391

Tower: Panelled base. 'Norwich' style 1S parapet with inset relief lozenges and small blank shields. Emblems over west entrance but flint missing.

## NORTH TUDDENHAM (32)     TG 056130

Tower: 1B parapet with proudwork panelling and quatrefoils, cf. Mattishall and Shipdham. Vertical chequer on buttresses.

## NORTH WALSHAM     TG 283304

South Porch: Two-stage base, blank shields above panelling. Feigned windows flanking central niche in upper stage of front and panelling in gable, both with ponderous stone elements. Panelled parapets on side walls.

## NORTHWOLD (14)      TF 765970

Tower:*     1S parapet with panelling and emblems. Panelling and emblems in base. Band of emblems over west door and emblems on buttresses.
Clerestory:     Blank three-light transomed feigned windows in proudwork between clerestory windows. Inscription over west window but flint missing.

## NORWICH, St Andrew's      TG 231087

Tower:     Pairs of rectangular panels on diagonal buttresses.
Chancel:     Panelling on base.

## NORWICH, St Benedict's (29)      TG 225088

Tower:     Round tower with octagonal belfry with brick flushwork feigned windows in diagonal faces. Tower only standing.

## NORWICH, St Clement's (58)      TG 232091

Tower:     'Norwich' style 1B parapet with inset relief lozenge emblems and small blank shields.

## NORWICH, St George's, Colegate      TG 230091

Tower:     'Norwich' style 1B parapet with inset relief lozenge emblems and blank shields. Remnants of panelling at side of tower door.

## NORWICH, St George's, Tombland      TG 233088

Tower:     'Norwich' style 1B parapet with inset plain lozenges and blank shields.
South Porch:     Two-storey. Panelling on base and foliations in front parapet.

## NORWICH, St Giles'      TG 226086

Tower:     1B parapet with panelling. Two courses of chequer below west window.

## NORWICH, St Gregory's      TG 228087

Tower:     1B parapet with proudwork panelling and quatrefoils.

### NORWICH, St John le Sepulchre           TG 234077

- Tower: 'Norwich' style 1B parapet with inset relief lozenge emblems and blank shields.
- North Porch: Two-storey, One band of emblems on front.

### NORWICH, St Lawrence's           TG 227088

- Tower: 1S parapet with panelling. Panels and relief emblems on base.
- South Aisle: Panelled base and dado of blank shields above, on two eastern bays.
- Chancel: Base and dado on south and east walls as south aisle.

### NORWICH, St Michael at Coslany (43)           TG 228090

- Tower: Panelling on base.
- South Aisle:* Panelled base. Wall decoration of feigned window tracery. Repeated quatrefoils in parapet.
- Chancel:* South wall similar to south aisle. East wall has panelled base, traceried feigned windows flanking the east window, encircled quatrefoils in the spandrels and two stages of panelling on the gable.

### NORWICH, St Michael at Plea           TG 232087

- South Porch: Two-storey. Crowned Ms over doorway. Emblems in plinth very worn.

### NORWICH, St Peter Mancroft           TG 229084

- Tower: Large panelling on lower stage. Panelled base continued round the whole church except at east end.

### NORWICH, St Stephen's           TG 229083

- Tower: A flushwork band of 'square' quatrefoils separates the knapped flint lower stage from an ashlar stone upper stage. A window above the north entrance rests on a band of shields set proud of their knapped flint background and has a band of chequer at its head. In each face of the upper stage, two-light flushwork feigned windows flank the belfry openings, above which are a flush knapped flint lozenge and two knapped flint circles.

### NORWICH, Erpingham Gate           TG 233089

- East Front: Three-stage panelling on big angle buttresses.

## NORWICH, Guildhall  TG 229086

East Wall:*     Upper stage is diagonal chequer. The shallow gable below the parapet is a chequer of triangles.

## NORWICH, St Ethelbert's Gate (46) (47) (48) (49)  TG 233088

West Front:*     Three feigned rose windows in the parapet with feigned two-light windows between. Two-course chequer band below upper-stage niches that are backed with squared flints.

East Front:*     Below the central upper window, a deep band of repeated four-petalled flower motifs. Flanking the window, feigned replicas, and above it a feigned rose window. In the spandrels, the four-petalled flower motif.

## OLD BUCKENHAM  TM 068915

Tower:*     Octagonal. Two-light Y-tracery feigned windows in the diagonals; the stonework of the mullions, tracery and arches is formed in the manner of true flushwork but the jambs have stones of varying widths – not strips.

North Aisle:     Emblems on buttresses.

## OLD CATTON  TG 231124

Tower:     Round tower with octagonal belfry has rectangular panels of flushwork defined in brick in the diagonal faces.

## ORMSBY ST MARGARET  TG 499145

Tower:     1S parapet with panelling. Panelled base.

## OVERSTRAND  TG 241408

Tower:     1B parapet with panelling.

South Porch:     Panelling on front and buttresses.

## OVINGTON  TF 925026

Tower:     A pair of panels below west window and each belfry window.

## PANXWORTH  TG 347135

Tower:     1B parapet with panelling.

plate 59. Poringland. Proudwork feigned windows in octagonal belfry.

**PENTNEY**            TF 721139

Tower:      1B parapet with rather irregular chequer of horizontal proportions.

**PLUMSTEAD**            TG 132350

Tower:      1B parapet with panelling of white knapped flint.

**PORINGLAND (59)**            TG 271017

Tower:      Round with octagonal belfry. Feigned two-light windows in proudwork in diagonals. These are not replicas of the belfry openings as usual, but have different tracery of the same pattern as Quidenham.

plate 60. Potter Heigham. Flushwork feigned window in octagonal belfry.

**POSTWICK**  TG 296078

Tower:* 1B parapet. Groups of three panel heads in merlons and two below indents; where they join, they rest on small shields in lieu of the normal mullions, cf. Barton Turf porch. Small blank shields between the panel heads. Panels on the bases of the diagonal buttresses, three on the face and five on the splays, have cinquefoiled shallow-sunk stone heads.

**POTTER HEIGHAM (60)**  TG 419199

Tower: Round tower with octagonal belfry stage of knapped flint with two-light feigned windows in diagonals. 1B parapet with panelling and emblems.

## PULHAM MARKET  TM 197861

- Tower: 1S parapet with panelling and quatrefoil emblems. Panelled base and buttresses.
- North Porch :* Two-storey. Panelling on west and front plinths. Four stages of panelling above plinth on front wall and two stages on diagonal buttresses.

## PULHAM ST MARY (45)  TM 212853

- Tower: 1B parapet with panelling.
- South Porch:* Two-storey. Panelled base on front and sides. Two stages of panelling on side walls; within each upper stage panel, the quatrefoil motif of the openwork stone parapet is reproduced in flushwork. Panelled buttresses, the lower panels with shallow-sunk stone heads with small relief carvings in their spandrels.

## QUIDENHAM  TM 028877

- Tower: Round tower with octagonal belfry. Two-light proudwork feigned windows in the diagonals replicating the belfry opening tracery.
- South Aisle: Emblems and panelling on buttresses.

## RACKHEATH  TG 270150

- Clerestory: A group of three panels only at each end of the clerestory.

## RANWORTH  TG 356148

- Tower: 1B parapet with panelling. Panelled base.
- Whole church: Panelled base, except on chancel.

## RAVENINGHAM  TM 398964

- Tower: Round tower with octagonal upper stage. Panelling and emblems in 1S parapet.

## REDENHALL (35) (XI)  TM 264844

- Tower:* 1S parapet with finialled panelling and emblems, the emblems in the east face in the form of miniature feigned rose windows. Polygonal stair turret at SE corner and polygonal buttresses have multi-stage panelling for their full height and are crowned at parapet level with turrets bearing two stages of finialled panels. West front entirely faced with bands of single- and double-width

|  |  |
|---|---|
| | panelling, with small fields of chequer above the second and third stage windows, straight chequer in the lower and diagonal in the upper. Belfry stages only of north and east fronts are fully panelled. |
| North Porch:* | Two-storey. Panelling on front and buttresses, and panelled base and parapet on front and side walls. |

## REEDHAM                                                         TG 428025

| | |
|---|---|
| Tower: | Panelling on base and buttresses. |

## REEPHAM                                                         TG 102229

### Two connected churches within one churchyard

**St Michael's** (West)

| | |
|---|---|
| Tower: | 1B parapet; rectangular panels in merlons have relief stone heads. Panelled base. |
| South Porch: | Remnants of panelling on base of side walls. Knapped flint gable crudely divided by stone strips. |

**St Mary's** (East)

| | |
|---|---|
| Tower: | 1B parapet with panelling. |

## RINGLAND                                                        TG 134141

| | |
|---|---|
| Tower:* | 1S parapet with panelling. The tops of the panels are cinquefoiled and within each panel there is a secondary finialled foliation, and in the merlons, a third order of foliations. The panels below the indent have a blank shield emblem surrounded by lobes. |
| South Porch: | Panelling on base of side walls and buttresses, the panels having an unusually wide, elongated, central lobe. Alternate panels have inset stone blank shields. |

## ROLLESBY                                                        TG 446158

| | |
|---|---|
| Tower: | Round tower with two octagonal upper stages. 1B parapet, chequered. |
| North Porch: | Panels on base of front. |
| South Aisle: | Panelled parapet. Vertical chequer on buttresses. |
| Chancel: | Wide rectangular flint panels on base with stone squares between. Vertical chequer on buttresses. |

## ROUDHAM                                                         TL 955873

| | |
|---|---|
| Tower: | A remnant of panelling in the parapet of the ruined tower. |

## ROUGHTON  TG 220366

Tower: Round tower. 1B parapet with simple brick flushwork panelling.

## ROYDON (near Diss)  TM 096804

Tower: Round tower with octagonal belfry stage. 1B parapet with panelling.

North Porch: Panelled base on front and on buttresses.

## RUNHAM  TG 460109

Tower: 2S parapet. Panelling and emblems in upper stage, the emblems crossed keys and crossed swords. Frieze of ashlar stone with inset knapped flint quatrefoils at intervals.

## RUSHFORD  TL 923812

South Porch: In the knapped flint gable which has brick dressings, each side of a central niche there is a pair of narrow flushwork panels and an inset relief stone emblem.

## SALLE  TG 110249

Parapets: Battlemented parapets on north and south porches, aisles, transepts, chancel and clerestory, with panelling in the merlons and quatrefoils below the indents.

## SANDRINGHAM  TF 692287

Tower: 1S parapet with carstone slips in lieu of knapped flint as infill to foliated panelling in merlons and steppings, and in emblems below indents.

South Porch: Two-storey. One canopied panel infilled with carstone, each side of arch.

## SAXLINGHAM NETHERGATE  TM 232972

Tower: 1B parapet with brick chequer flushwork with squares of one-brick size. Five narrow panels each side of west door, level with the arch stage.

South Porch: Panelling on face of buttresses only.

## SCARNING  TF 954122

Tower: Panelled base of proudwork on south and west sides, flushwork on north.

## SCOLE  TM 151791

   Tower:       1B parapet with chequer.

## SCOTTOW  TG 265238

   Tower:       Panelled base. 1B parapet with panelling.
   South Porch:   Two-storey. Panelled parapet on front and side walls.

## SHADWELL PARK HOUSE  TL 929831
### (not open to the public)

   East Tower:    Panelling on upper stage.
   Tower Stair
     Turret:     Panelled.
   Stable Yard:   Panelling around low wall of central feature.

## SHELFANGER  TM 108837

   Tower:       1B parapet with chequer.

## SHIMPLING  TM 156827

   Tower:       Round tower with octagonal belfry of brick and flint. Feigned windows in the diagonal faces.

## SHIPDHAM  TF 958075

   Tower:       1B parapet with panelling and quatrefoils in proudwork, cf. North Tuddenham and Mattishall.

## SHROPHAM  TL 984928

   Tower:       Chequer on wide diagonal buttresses.
   Chancel:    Single proudwork panel on buttresses, but panel heads cemented.

## SOUTHBURGH  TG 003048

   Tower:       1B parapet with panelling and quatrefoils in merlons. Single course chequer base.
   South Porch:   Diagonal chequer in gable peak.

## SOUTH CREAKE  TF 855363

   South Porch:   Emblems in gable and side parapets.

## SOUTH LOPHAM    TM 039818

Tower: 1B parapet. Merlons vertically divided into two plain rectangular panels. One foliated panel below each indent.
Clerestory: Single emblems between windows on south side.

## SOUTHREPPS    TG 257368

Tower: Panelled base frieze. 1B parapet with emblems. Paired panels each side of west door. Proudwork panelling on buttresses.

## SOUTH WALSHAM    TG 365133

Tower: 1B parapet with panelling.
South Porch: Two-storey. Panelled base on front and buttresses. Pair of panels each side of arch.

## SPARHAM    TG 071197

Tower: 1B parapet with two-stage panelling.

## SPORLE    TF 850115

Tower: 1B parapet with proudwork panelling on three sides.

## STALHAM    TG 373252

South Porch: Panelling on front up to arch springing level only.
Clerestory: Feigned two-light windows inset between widely-spaced windows.

## STANFORD    TL 857947

Tower: Round tower with octagonal belfry stage. Feigned proudwork two-light windows in diagonals.

## STARSTON    TM 234844

Tower: 1B parapet with straight chequer on the east face, but diagonal on south, west and north.
South Aisle: Diagonal chequer parapet.

## STIFFKEY    TF 974430

Tower: Chequer base (poor). Some vertical chequer on buttresses.

plate 61. Thompson. Rectangular chequer on tower base.

|     |     |
| --- | --- |
| North Porch: | Panelling on front up to gable level, and on base of buttresses. |
| Nave: | Level parapets with five courses of chequer on north side and four on south. Vertical chequer on buttresses. |

## STODY                                           TG 056351

Tower:         Round tower with circular 1B parapet with panelling.

## STRUMPTSHAW                   TG 349078

Tower:         1B parapet with panelling.

## SUFFIELD                                TG 233313

Tower:         Three-course square chequer base and on buttresses. Vertical chequer on buttresses.

## SUSTEAD                                 TG 183370

South Porch:   Remnants of inset crosses botonée each side of arch.

## SWAFIELD                               TG 287331

Tower:         1B parapet with panels in merlons and quatrefoils below indents.

## SWANNINGTON (26)   TG 134194

South Porch:*   Over the arch, IHS NAZARENUS in Lombardic script. Lombardic initials in base on front and buttresses.

## SWANTON MORLEY   TG 019173

Tower:   1B parapet has proudwork panelling with flat chamfered stonework and angular, gable-shaped panel-heads. Proudwork panelling on the bases of the west wall and buttresses has moulded stonework.
Aisles:   Proudwork base, as on tower, continues on west wall and corner buttresses. Side and east walls have a one-course base of chequer rectangles.
South Porch:   Chequer squares in base on front.

## SWARDESTON   TM 199025

Tower:   1B parapet with panelling and emblems.

## TAVERHAM   TG 160139

Tower:   Round tower with octagonal belfry stage. Octagonal 1B parapet with panelling.

## THARSTON   TM 190943

Tower:   1B parapet with panelling.
North Porch:   Panelling on front and panelled base on front and sides.

## THETFORD  St Peter's   TL 869832

Tower:   Large buttresses with chequer.
Nave:   Emblems on plinth of three east bays and the two buttresses between, but very worn and flint missing. Emblems on south wall buttresses, most flint missing.
Chancel:   Inscriptions and emblems on plinth of south wall but all flint missing.

## THOMPSON (61)   TL 930970

Tower:*   Base of three courses of horizontally rectangular chequer infilled with small squared knapped flints. 1B parapet with panelling.

## THORNHAM   TF 734435

Tower:   Proudwork panelled base and proudwork panels on faces of angle buttresses.

## THORPE ABBOTTS　　　　　　　　　　　　　　　TM 187789

　Tower:　　　　Round tower with octagonal belfry. Feigned windows in diagonal faces.

## THORPE ST ANDREW, Norwich　　　　　　　　　TG 261085

　Old church:
　Tower:　　　　1B parapet with proudwork panels.

## THRIGBY　　　　　　　　　　　　　　　　　　TG 460124

　Tower:　　　　1B parapet with panelling.

## THURLTON　　　　　　　　　　　　　　　　　TM 416984

　Tower:*　　　Diagonal chequer base and on buttresses. Panelled dado. Single-stage level parapet with panelling.

## THWAITE　　　　　　　　　　　　　　　　　　TG 193335

　South Aisle:　Proudwork panelling on buttresses.

## TIBENHAM　　　　　　　　　　　　　　　　　TM 135899

　Tower:　　　　1B parapet with panelling and emblems. Diagonal chequer base.

## TIVETSHALL ST MARGARET　　　　　　　　　　TM 163870

　Tower:　　　　1B parapet with panelling.

## TOFT MONKS　　　　　　　　　　　　　　　　TM 427954

　Tower:　　　　Octagonal tower. Octagonal 1B parapet with panelling and emblems.
　South Porch:　Panelling on front.

## TOPCROFT　　　　　　　　　　　　　　　　　TM 266929

　Tower:　　　　Round tower with three octagonal upper stages. Two-light feigned windows in diagonal faces of belfry stage.

## TRUNCH　　　　　　　　　　　　　　　　　　TG 287349

　Tower:　　　　Single-stage level parapet with cinquefoil panelling in white flint.

## TUNSTEAD      TG 308227

    Clerestory:    Low windowless clerestory with blank arcading from end to end with quatrefoils between the panel heads. White knapped flint.

## UPPER SHERINGHAM      TG 145419

    Tower:    1B parapet with panels in merlons and quatrefoils below indents.

## WALCOTT      TG 360318

    Tower:    Panelled base. 1S parapet, unusually with three steppings, i.e. thirteen zones, panelled.

## WARHAM ST MARY      TF 944417

    Tower:    1B parapet with diagonal chequer.

## WAXHAM      TG 440263

    Tower:    Single-stage level parapet with rectangular panels.

## WEASENHAM ALL SAINTS      TF 849214

    South Porch:    Small proudwork panelling in base. Brownish knapped flints.

## WEASENHAM ST PETER      TF 856224

    North Porch:    Panelling on front.
    Nave:    Proudwork panelled base, same as on porch at All Saints.

## WELLS NEXT THE SEA      TF 918432

    Tower:    1B parapet with proudwork panelling. Vertical chequer on buttresses.
    Aisles:    Vertical chequer on buttresses.

## WENDLING      TF 931131

    Tower:    1B parapet with panelling.

## WEST BILNEY      TF 716153

    Tower:    1B parapet with panelling, panels with simple semi-circular heads.

## WEST BRADENHAM  TF 917092

Tower: 1B parapet with chequer.

## WESTFIELD  TF 993099

South Porch: Chequer up to arch springing level, with plain vertical bands in gable.

## WEST HARLING  TL 974852

Tower: Diagonal chequer on base on south and west; square chequer on north, the upper course of rectangles. Bases of the diagonal buttresses have similar chequer to north wall base. Square and vertical chequer on buttresses.

## WESTON LONGVILLE  TG 113159

South Porch: Panelling on front.
Clerestory:* Quatrefoil windows are framed in flat stone squares with flush knapped flint infilling in the corners.

## WEST SOMERTON (3)  TG 475196

Tower:* Round tower with octagonal belfry stage. In the diagonal faces, feigned replicas of the lancet belfry openings, their stone dressings built conventionally and infilled flush with squared knapped flint. An early precursor of flushwork.

## WEST TOFTS  TL 836929

Tower: Base with panelling, inscriptions and emblems including several lily-in-vase motifs but most flint missing.

## WESTWICK  TG 286260

Tower: 1B parapet with 'Norwich' style panelling in light flints. Plinth has stone relief lozenges of knapped flint alternating with relief stone panels.

## WEST WINCH  TF 633159

Tower: Panelled base and large trefoiled panels flanking west door, and on buttresses.
South Porch:* South front and diagonal buttresses chequer. Gable peak flint/brick chequer where 1706 sundial inset.

## WEYBOURNE  TG 112431

Tower: 1B parapet; panelling with slightly recessed flintwork and shallow-sunk stone panel heads. Panels and emblems on base of buttresses.

South Porch:* Two-storey with chequer of red bricks and white flints above arch. Chequer squares one-brick size.

## WHISSONSETT  TF 919234

Tower: 1B parapet, with shallow-sunk stone head panels.

## WICKHAMPTON  TG 427055

Tower: 1S parapet with shallow-sunk stone head panels

## WICKLEWOOD  TG 070024

Buttresses: Chequer, three squares wide.

## WICKMERE  TG 165338

Tower: Round tower with circular 1B parapet with panelling.

South Porch:* Two-storey. Flushwork panelling on bases of front and buttresses and on gable. Proudwork panelling on rest of front and buttresses. White squared knapped flint.

Clerestory:* Botonée crosses inset within roughly-squared white knapped flint, between the windows.

## WIGGENHALL ST GERMANS  TF 597140

Tower: Stone tower. 1S parapet with shallow proudwork panels in merlons and steppings with emblems below indents. The infilling is mostly now in brick.

## WINTERTON  TG 491196

Tower: 1S parapet with proudwork panelling. Panelled base surmounted by dado of five courses of five-inch chequer.

South Porch: Panelled base on front and side walls.

## WIVETON  TG 044428

Tower: 1B parapet with panelling and emblems.

Chancel:* Each side of east window, pairs of panels in two stages with quatrefoils between the stages. South wall bears the remnants of similar panelling. Panelling on diagonal buttresses at east end.

plate 62. Wymondham. Proudwork in east bays of north clerestory.

## WOODBASTWICK  TG 332152

Tower: 1B parapet with panelling.

## WOOD DALING  TG 090270

Tower: 1B parapet with panelling in merlons and blank shields below indents on east and north faces only. Two-course chequer base.

## WOODTON  TM 285946

Tower: Round tower with octagonal upper stage and panelled 1B parapet.

## WORSTEAD (36)  TG 302261

Tower:* Also on tower buttresses, two-stage base with flushwork panelling below a course of relief stonework quatrefoils, and above this, a dado stage of flushwork blank arcading with ornate traceried panel heads.

| | |
|---|---|
| South Porch:* | Two-storey. Two-stage base on front, sides, buttresses and stair turret comprising panelling below a course of rather disjointed wavy tracery motifs and quatrefoils. Each side of central triple niches on the upper stage of the front, a feigned window. The front parapet is panelled and the side parapets chequered. All re-entrant angles between the angle buttresses and walls have panelled splays. |
| South Aisle: | Two-stage base of panelling below quatrefoils. Level panelled parapet. |
| North Aisle: | Similar to south aisle but much flint missing. |

## WRETHAM, St Lawrence (formerly East Wretham)   TL 900915

| | |
|---|---|
| Tower: | Ruin. Octagonal belfry stage on square tower has feigned windows in diagonal faces. 1B parapet with panelling. |

## WROXHAM   TG 296176

| | |
|---|---|
| Tower: | 1B parapet with panelling. |

## WYMONDHAM (62)   TG 107015

| | |
|---|---|
| West Tower: | Band of chequer about halfway up. Proudwork panelling on buttresses above the level of the chequer band. |
| North Clerestory:* | Flushwork panelling except the two east bays which have proudwork. |

# SUFFOLK

## ALDERTON   TM 343417

| | |
|---|---|
| Tower: | Ruined. Traces of panelling over west door. |
| North Porch: | Chequer base and panelling on front. Emblems in base on side walls. |

## BACTON   TM 053672

| | |
|---|---|
| South Porch: | Panelling in base on front and sides. |
| Clerestory: | Emblems between windows, one above and one below the string course. Panels at each end. Small flushwork triangles between north clerestory window arches. |

## BADINGHAM   TM 305683

| | |
|---|---|
| South Porch: | Emblems in base on front and sides. Panelled front. Emblems in front parapet, panelling in side parapets. |

## BADWELL ASH               TL 989690

Tower:* 1S parapet. Inscription in Gothic script in steppings, plain panelling below, and quatrefoil variations below indents. Emblems in base.

South Porch:* Emblems in base on front and sides. Panelled front. Front and side parapets panelled with emblems below indents.

## BARDWELL               TL 941737

Tower: Chequer base.

South Porch: Chequer base. Panelled front. Front and side parapets panelled. Many panels have shallow-sunk stone heads – probably repairs.

## BARHAM               TM 137509

Tower: 1S parapet. Ashlar stone with knapped flint quatrefoils inset at intervals.

## BARSHAM (Frontispiece)               TM 397897

Chancel:* East wall entirely patterned with a criss-cross of diagonal stone strips forming a lattice of diamonds infilled with knapped flint. This trellis theme is extended across the east window by diagonal mullions which continue the lines of the stonework strips.

## BECCLES               TM 421905

North Porch:* Two-storey. Panelled front, the panels in the two lower stages of the shallow-sunk stone head type. Front and side parapets panelled.

Chancel: Panelling dado across east end and a band of quatrefoils below the east window.

## BEDFIELD               TM 227664

Tower: 1B parapet with panels in merlons and emblems and chequer in indents. Panelled base and buttresses.

## BELTON               TG 486029

South Porch: Panelling on front.

## BENACRE               TM 512845

Tower: 1B parapet. In each face, three squares of tracery-based flushwork inset within flint cobble background.

## BENHALL  TM 372619

Tower: 1S parapet with panelling and quatrefoils.

## BILDESTON  TL 991495

Tower: Panelled base.
South Porch: Panelled front and buttresses.

## BLAXHALL  TM 357569

Tower: Panelled base but most flint replaced with brick. Band of quatrefoils alternating with small panels over blocked west door. Panelled buttresses.

## BLYFORD  TM 424768

Tower: 1S parapet with panelling and emblems. Panelled base and buttresses. Band of quatrefoils over west door.
North Porch: Panelled front with emblem base. The design of the front is generally similar to the porches at Halesworth and Huntingfield: features common to all three are the relief stone parapet with wavy tracery and the small quatrefoils below panelling stages in relief stonework or flushwork. Flushwork wavy tracery in side wall parapets echoes the similar relief decoration of the front parapet, cf. Ufford.

## BLYTHBOROUGH  TM 450753

Tower: 1B parapet with panelling and emblems.
South Porch: Two-storey. Panelled buttresses and a band of diagonal chequer below openwork parapet.
Aisles: Panelled buttresses with chequer and emblems on base. Band of diagonal chequer below openwork parapet.
Chancel:* Three bays of panelling in three stages surmounted by emblems, each side of east window. Below, fourteen symbols, twelve of which are crowned Lombardic letters, each in an individual flushwork square.

## BOTESDALE, Chapel-of-Ease  TM 049759

Nave: Three-line inscription on a stone panel in the knapped flint wall over the N. door, the central part obliterated by a later inserted window.

## BRAMFORD  TM 127463

Tower: Three courses of chequer all round base.

North Porch: A little panelling on buttresses.
North Vestry: Panels on one stage of diagonal buttresses.

## BRAMPTON        TM 434816

Tower: 1B parapet with panelling and emblems. Panelling and vertical chequer on buttresses.

## BRANDESTON        TM 248602

Tower: 1S parapet with panelling.

## BREDFIELD        TM 269530

Tower: 1S parapet with panelling, the flint panels mostly renewed in brick. Sub-course of knapped flint and square brick-tiles laid diagonally. Panelled base on south and north, emblems on west. Panelling on buttresses.

## BROCKLEY        TL 827556

Tower: Panelled base, except on south which has an inscription in Gothic script originally apparently flushwork but flint now lost. Panels and emblems on buttresses.

plate 63. St Mary's, Bungay. Crowned 'MARIA' monograms above tower west window.

## BROME (33)            TM 145765

| | |
|---|---|
| South Porch: | Panelled front including base and parapet. The flintwork of all panels is recessed about ¼", much less than normal proudwork. East wall parapet has panelling and emblems but on the west modern repairs have left just rectangular panels. |
| Nave: | Panelling and emblems in base. Panelling in parapet with cresting in base of panels. Large panelled buttress at south-east corner. |
| Chancel: | Panelling in parapet. |
| Transept: | Panelling in parapet. |
| North Aisle: | Sunk flint quatrefoils in stone parapet. |

## BROMESWELL            TM 303507

| | |
|---|---|
| Tower: | 1S parapet with panelling. Panelled base and buttresses. |

## BRUNDISH            TM 271695

| | |
|---|---|
| South Porch: | Panelled front. |
| Chancel: | Chequer base on buttresses. |

## BUNGAY, Holy Trinity            TM 338898

| | |
|---|---|
| Tower: | Round tower with octagonal 1B parapet with panelling. |
| South Porch: | Panelling in parapets of front and side walls, with relief emblems. |

## BUNGAY, St Mary's (63)            TM 337898

| | |
|---|---|
| Tower:* | Panelled base. Three-stage panelling on the two lower stages of the polygonal buttresses. A row of eight crowned Marian monograms follow the arch curvature over the west window. |

## BURES            TL 907340

| | |
|---|---|
| South Chapel: | Panels in merlons, emblems in indents of battlemented parapet of east wall. |

## BURGH            TM 223523

| | |
|---|---|
| Tower: | 1B parapet with panelling. |

## BURY ST EDMUNDS CATHEDRAL  TL 856642

   Tower parapet: Pairs of panels in merlons. Lombardic E emblem below indents.
   Chancel
     Clerestory: Above a string course at window tracery level, finialled panels between the windows with diagonal chequer over the window arches; battlemented parapet above with quatrefoils in the merlons.
   South Chapel: Bands of alternating pointed trefoils above the windows; battlemented parapet with pairs of panels in the merlons.
   South Transept: Gable wall: Panels below a string course, above which alternating horizontal bands of knapped flint and stone, with panels in the gable. Sides: Diagonal chequer at window tracery level; battlemented parapet with panels in merlons and a diamond and triangles below indents.
   North Transept: Gable wall similar to south transept, but simpler.
   North Transept
     Annex: Two tall semi-circular blank arches, each divided below a chequer tympanum into a pair of blank pointed arches faced with alternating bands of knapped flint and stone.

This flushwork is all on the cathedral extensions dating from the 1960s. Tower completed in 2004.

## BUTLEY  TM 373502

   Tower: 1S parapet with panelling.

## BUTLEY, Priory Gatehouse (in private grounds)  TM 377495

   North Front:* Rising between truncated projecting bays that were formerly the medieval gatehouse towers, the central gabled façade has tracery-based curvilinear flushwork over the two entrance archways, and feigned windows flanking the central upper window; between, rows of armorial bearings in relief stonework form a chequer pattern with squares of knapped flint each containing a smaller stone square bearing a relief fleur-de-lys. The projecting bays each have a flushwork feigned window and a panel of chequer on their inner flank walls.

## BUXHALL  TM 003577

   Tower: Panelled base and chequer on buttresses.
   North Porch: Chequer on front and side parapets.

## CAMPSEA ASH　　　　　　　　　　　　　　　　　　　TM 330559

Tower: 1B parapet with panelling in merlons and emblems below indents. Base and buttresses panelled. Band of quatrefoils over west door.

## CARLTON COLVILLE　　　　　　　　　　　　　　　　TM 510902

Tower: 1S parapet with panelling.

## CAVENDISH (XIV)　　　　　　　　　　　　　　　　　TL 805465

Clerestory:* Without a string course at window arch level, the flushwork between the windows extends for the full height of the clerestory up to the parapet and comprises two-stage panelling, four panels wide, with the upper panels paired under finialled canopy heads. The horizontal division between the two stages aligns with the intermediate transome of the tall three-light windows, and the tracery in the heads of the upper panels occurs at the same level as the window tracery, thus establishing a satisfying relationship between the architecture and the decoration. The battlemented parapet has panelling in the merlons and blank shields surrounded by foliations below the indents.

Chancel: Chequer on the base.

## CHARSFIELD　　　　　　　　　　　　　　　　　　　TM 254566

Tower: 1S parapet with panelling on brick tower. Emblems in plinth but flint missing.

plate 64. Sequences of repeated motifs between the merlons of the crenellated parapet on the south aisle of Coddenham church.

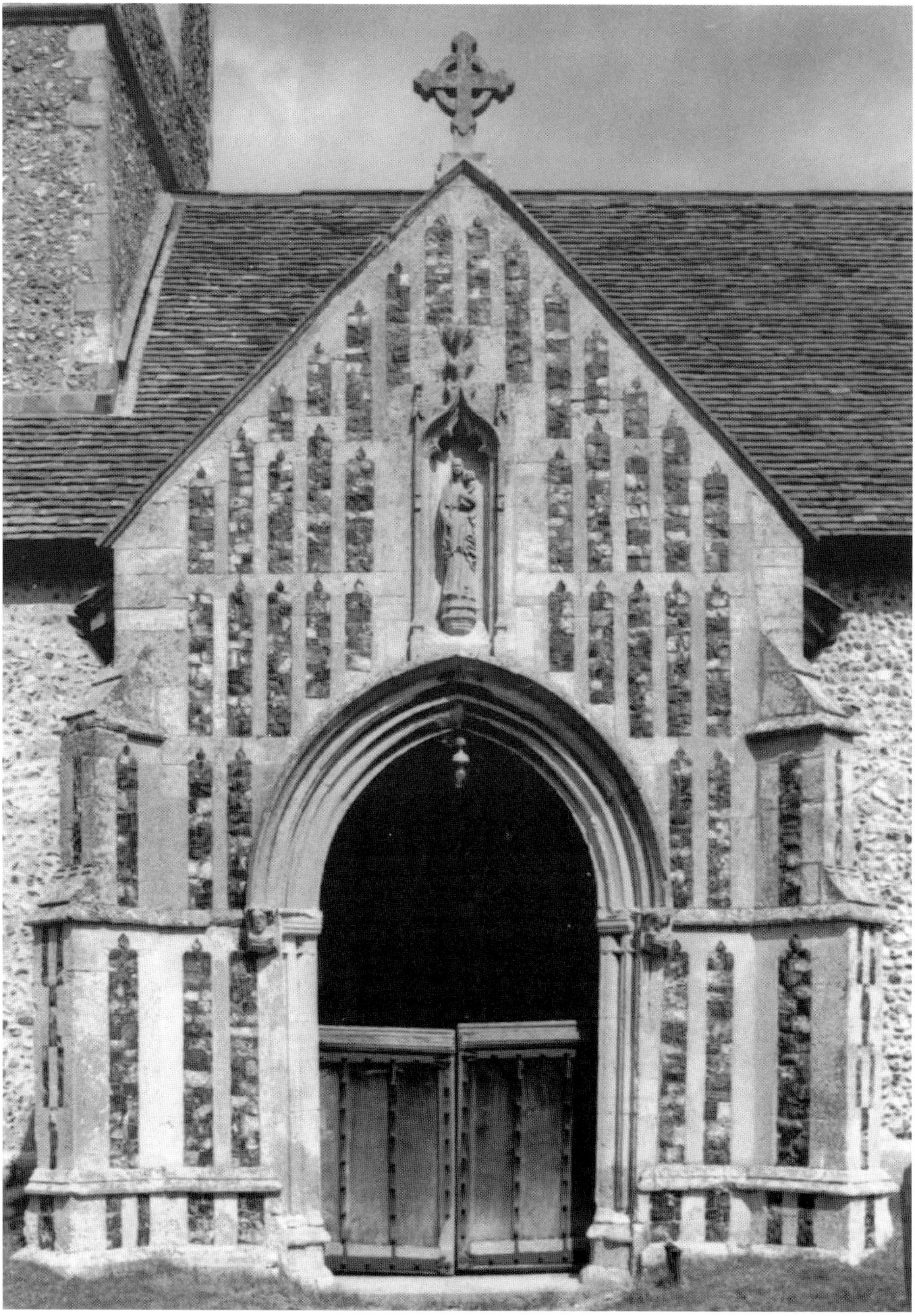

South Porch: Brick. Stone flushwork emblems in base on front and panelling in base of side walls.

## CHEDISTON                                            TM 358778

Tower: 1B parapet with panelling and emblems.

## CHEVINGTON                                           TL 789601

Tower: Panelling in base and proudwork panelling on buttresses.

## COCKFIELD                                            TL 903550

Tower: 1B parapet with chequer. Chequer also on buttresses. Rectangular panelling on base.
South Porch: Chequer base on front and sides and on buttresses. Some panelling on front at sides of arch and in a band above.

## CODDENHAM (64)                                       TM 133542

Tower: 1S parapet with panelling.
North Porch: One band of panels on front.
Clerestory: Two stages of panelling between windows separated by a string course. Above windows, blank shields on lobed background and tracery motifs but most flint missing. Parapet on north side only has emblems and running wavy plant forms but all flint missing.
South Aisle:* Battlemented parapet has pairs of panels in merlons, with ribbons of cresting, alternating pointed trefoils and quatrefoil variations between.

## COMBS                                                TM 051569

Tower: Chequer on base.

## COPDOCK                                              TM 120415

Tower: Panelling on base and buttresses. Row of panels above west door.
Nave: Panelled base on north and south walls and west wall of north transept, matching tower.
South Porch: Panelled base on west and south walls.

## CORTON                                               TM 539981

Tower: 1S parapet with panelling. Rectangular panels in base. Panelled buttresses.

plate 65. Creeting St Mary. A simple flushwork panelling scheme on the gabled south porch.

South Porch: Three-course small chequer on base of front and buttresses; one course normal chequer on side walls.

## COTTON  TM 070669

South Porch: Panelling on front and emblems in parapet.
South
  Clerestory:* Single emblems above string course between closely-spaced windows. Brick voussoirs alternating with knapped flint in window arches. Composite rectangle of features at west end.
North
  Clerestory: Panelling.

## COVEHITHE  TM 523818

South Aisle: In ruins. Rectangular chequer base surmounted by dado of panelling.

## CREETING ST MARY (65)  TM 094567

Tower: 1B parapet with panelling.
South Porch:* Panelling on front and buttresses. Panels in gable nicely varied in height to suit the wall shape.

## CRETINGHAM  TM 228606

Tower: 1S parapet with panelling.

## DALHAM (44)  TL 725625

Tower:* 1B parapet with inscriptions in Roman lettering:
South: KEEPE MY SABBATHS
West:: DEO TRIN VNI SACRVM
North: ANNO DOMINI 1625
East: REVERENCE MY SANCTVARY
The base is black knapped flint with a central feature in each face formed with diagonal stone and flint squares. The faces of unusually wide diagonal buttresses are profusely decorated with chequer motifs, several types of cross and other unusual devices. At about halfway up the belfry stage, the diagonal buttresses become transformed into clasping buttresses and have proudwork panelling.

## DARSHAM  TM 421699

Tower: 2S parapet with panelling in upper stage and diagonal chequer in the frieze.

plate 66. Flushwork emblems and panelling in the two-stage parapet of the tower at Earl Stonham.

### DEBENHAM  TM 174632

South Aisle: Panelling on buttresses with very precise squared flintwork. Victorian.

### DENNINGTON  TM 281670

Tower: One course of squares on base.
North Porch: Base on front as on tower. Panelling up to arch springing level only.
Nave: Chequer on buttresses.

### DUNWICH, Friary  TM 478704

Ruins: Panelling above a doorway in wall near former gatehouse.

### EARL SOHAM  TM 237633

Tower: 1S parapet with panelling. Panelling on base and buttresses.

### EARL STONHAM (40)(66)  TM 107589

Tower:* 2S parapet with panelling and blank shields in the upper stage, and varied quatrefoil emblems with single panels between in the frieze. Panelled base and buttresses.
Clerestory:* Four panels between each window, in two stages separated by the string course at window-arch springing level. Finialled heads to lower panels and simple trefoiled heads to upper.

## EAST BERGHOLT                                          TM 070344

| | |
|---|---|
| Tower: | Some panelling on incomplete tower. |
| Aisles: | Panelling on base and buttresses. |
| Chancel: | Panelling on base. |

## EASTON                                                      TM 283588

| | |
|---|---|
| Tower: | 1S panelled parapet on octagonal top of square tower. |

## ELMSWELL (5) (9) (13)                            TL 982637

| | |
|---|---|
| Tower:* | 1S parapet with two-stage panelling and emblems below the indents. Emblems on base and buttresses. |
| South Aisle: | Emblems on buttresses. Strident and incongruous c.19 chequer composition on east end. |

## ELVEDEN                                            TL 823799

| | |
|---|---|
| West Tower: | Panelling on base with a course of chequer above. |
| South Tower: | Panelling dado with quatrefoils above and below; triangular chequer frieze above the arch extends round all sides; below the belfry openings on the south, an inscription in Gothic script takes the place of a band of quatrefoils on the other sides. An octagonal turret at the north-west corner terminates with a quatrefoil in each facet. |
| N.Nave and Chancel: | Triangular chequer frieze below parapets and on west gable. Two pairs of traceried panels each side of east window. |

## EYE                                                           TM 149738

| | |
|---|---|
| Tower:* | Of generally similar design to Redenhall and Laxfield, the four-stage tower has polygonal buttresses with multi-stage panelling on their three lower stages. The west front is entirely faced with bands of panelling, the panels in some of the bands in the two lower stages being half width. A small panel of chequer below the third-stage window. On the south, east and north of the tower the belfry stages only are panelled like the west. |
| South Porch:* | Two-storey. Four stages of panelling on the side walls; the panel infilling is brick, probably replacing original knapped flint. Emblems in base but flint missing. |
| Chancel: | Panelling surmounted by an emblem between the chancel clerestory windows on the south side only. Fine emblems and panelling on faces of c.19 buttresses at east end. |

## FALKENHAM                                              TM 293391

Tower: 1S parapet, panelled. Twin two-light belfry openings have a pair of slender panels between and an emblem below each light. Single inset emblem in centre of each wall just below parapet. Emblems in base of south-west and north-west buttresses.

Aisles: Panelling and emblems in south parapet and mainly chequer in north.
North Vestry: Panelling and emblems in parapet.

## FELSHAM                                                TL 947570

North Porch:* Panelled front and parapet. Panelled base on side walls. cf. Hitcham.
Nave: Panelling on battlemented parapets.

## FINNINGHAM (16)                                        TM 066695

Tower: Knapped flint infill to west door spandrels.
South Porch: Panelled front; shallow-sunk foliations on the stone heads of panels in the main stage; the sinkings above three front panels and over two on the buttresses are carved on single stones.

## FORNHAM ALL SAINTS                                     TL 837677

South Aisle: Paired panels in merlons alternating with emblems below indents of battlemented parapet.

## FORNHAM ST MARTIN                                      TL 852669

Tower: 1B parapet with chequer. Chequer base.

## FRAMLINGHAM                                            TM 285636

Tower: 2B parapet with emblems in frieze below relief stone upper stage. Emblems and panels in base.
Clerestory: Four panels between windows, the centre ones shorter, with emblem above.

## FRAMSDEN                                               TM 200598

Tower: 1B parapet with quatrefoils and panels. Panelled base and buttresses. Band of alternating panels and relief stone shields over west door.
South Aisle: Panelling on base and on the stepped parapet of the west wall.

plate 67. Gipping. Central window in the nave south wall with emblems and panelling on the unusual central mullion.

| South Porch: | West wall aligns with the west wall of the south aisle, separated by a panelled buttress. Panelled base and stepped parapet on sides and front continue those of the aisle west wall. Panelled front with a band of small quatrefoils below the upper stage of panelling. |

## FRESSINGFIELD                                   TM 261775

| South Porch: | Two-storey. Panelled base on front and side walls. Panelled front and buttresses with castellations on the intermediate stone heads between panelling stages. |
| South Aisle: | Chequer on buttresses. |

## GEDDING                                         TL 952582

| Tower: | Emblems on face of buttresses include an unusual motif. |

## GIPPING (67)                                    TM 072636

| Nave and Chancel:* | Panelling on wide mullion between lights of central window in north and south nave walls, with circular |

|  |  |
|---|---|
|  | emblems in the spandrels. Proudwork panels each side of central doorways. Panelling and many emblems on buttresses but much flint missing from emblems. |
| North Annex: | Feigned bay window in proudwork with flushwork emblems and panelling below. |

## GISLEHAM                                    TM 514886

| South Porch: | Panelled plinth on front, east side and diagonal buttresses. Chequer in angle between front wall and buttresses. Inset shallow-relief stone panels in front parapet. |
|---|---|

## GLEMSFORD                                    TL 834484

| South Porch:* | Front: panelled base and simple panelling each side of archway. Battlemented parapet panelled. Side walls: panelled base, two-stage panelling the upper stage panels paired under finialled canopy heads with blank shields between. Battlemented panelled parapet. |
|---|---|
| South Aisle and South Chapel:* | Generally similar flushwork to that on the porch side walls. |
| North Side: | Heavily restored and only a little flushwork remains. |

## GOSBECK                                    TM 150557

| Tower: | Deep 1S parapet with panelling and chequer. |
|---|---|
| North Vestry: | Parapet panelled with brick flushwork. |

## GREAT ASHFIELD                                    TL 996678

| Tower: | Panelled base on buttresses and west wall only. |
|---|---|
| South Porch:* | Brick flushwork on front and on base of side walls. |
| South Aisle: | Emblems on buttresses. |

## GREAT BARTON (XVI)                                    TL 890660

| Tower:* | 2S parapet with panelling and emblems in upper stage: circle-based emblems and wavy tracery in frieze. |
|---|---|
| South Porch: | Brick panelling flushwork base on side walls. |

## GREAT BEALINGS                                    TM 231489

| Tower: | Panelling and emblems on buttresses and on 1S parapet. |
|---|---|
| North Porch: | Brick panelling flushwork base on side walls. |

## GREAT GLEMHAM                           TM 340617

Tower:         1B parapet with panelling. Panelling on buttresses.
North Porch:   Panelling on base on front and side walls.

## GREAT WALDINGFIELD                      TL 912439

Tower:         Chequer base. Vertical chequer on buttresses.
South Porch:   Chequer base on side walls. 5-lozenge emblem on buttresses.
Aisles:        Chequer base.
South
  Clerestory:  Inscription in parapet merlons. Flint missing.

## GREAT WENHAM                            TM 071381

Tower:         Buttresses panelled with unusual plain shallow-pitched angle-headed panels.

## GRUNDISBURGH (11)                       TM223511

South
  Clerestory:  Emblems between windows above string course include lily-in-vase motif.

plate 68. Halesworth. Supermullioned cinquefoiled panels in the merlons, and quatrefoil emblems below the indents in the tower parapet.

## HALESWORTH (24) (68)  TM 386774

Tower:* 1B parapet with panelling and multi-quatrefoil emblems. Panelled base. Band of quatrefoils over west door. Panelled buttresses.

North Porch: Panelled front and buttresses. The overall design is generally similar to that of porches at Blyford and Huntingfield.

## HAWSTEAD (15)  TL 855593

Tower:* 1S parapet with panelling and emblems. Base: unusual geometrical emblems on west face, and panelling on north and south.

## HELMINGHAM  TM 191577

Tower:* 1S parapet with panelling surmounted by emblems incorporating shields on lobed background. Some shields are blank, some contain flushwork devices and one bears the date 1543. The base contains an inscription but all the flint is gone. A ribbon of emblems above the west door includes a lily-in-vase, but most of the flint is missing. Panelled buttresses.

South Porch: The front has a panelled gable with a delicate little composition of circles and half-circles in the gable peak. Panelled base and parapet on side walls.

## HENLEY  TM 159513

Tower: Panelling on buttresses.

## HENSTEAD  TM 488861

Tower: 1B parapet with panelling and emblems.
South Porch: Panelled base on front and buttresses.

## HESSET  TL 937618

Tower: Three-course chequer base.
South Porch: Emblems on buttresses and front and side plinths, but insensitively pointed.

## HINDERCLAY  TM 027769

Tower: 1S parapet with unusual arrangement of panels and emblems although, except on west face, callously repaired. Dummy lights below the two-light belfry openings are each infilled with a chequer of eight squares except on the east where the infill is rubble flint. Rectangular upright panels on base.

## HITCHAM (38)  TL 984510

| | |
|---|---|
| Tower: | Chequer base. |
| South Porch:* | Panelling on front and on angle buttresses. Panelled base and parapet on side walls. cf. Felsham. |
| Clerestory: | Battlemented chequer parapet. |

## HOLLESLEY  TM 353444

| | |
|---|---|
| Tower: | 1S parapet with panelling and emblems. Panelling on base and buttresses. |
| Chancel: | Panelling on buttresses. |

## HONINGTON  TL 913746

| | |
|---|---|
| South Porch: | Panelling on front; battlemented parapet with emblems in merlons and below indents. Band of quatrefoils above the base on side walls. Most flushwork on side parapets has been replaced with brick. All the flushwork is spoiled by recent insensitive pointing. |

## HOPTON (IV)  TL 994790

| | |
|---|---|
| Tower:* | Chequer on classical belfry stage built on medieval lower part. |

## HORHAM (69)  TM 210725

| | |
|---|---|
| Tower:* | 1S parapet with exuberant panelling and emblems similar to Helmingham. Flushwork emblem infills within proudwork squares below belfry openings. Panelled base with infill of flint rubble nodules. Panelled buttresses. |

## HORRINGER  TL 825620

| | |
|---|---|
| Tower: | 1B parapet with chequer of large squares (1912). |
| South Porch: | Panelling on front with chequer in gable. |
| Nave: | Parapet chequer of large squares (1912). |

## HOXNE  TM 181775

| | |
|---|---|
| Tower: | 1S parapet with panelling in merlons, pointed quatrefoil with fleur-de-lys finial in steppings and blank shields below indents. Panelled buttresses. |

plate 69. Horham. Nodular rubble flint infill in the panels on the tower base.

Buttresses: Rectangular panels on bases of nave, chancel and porch buttresses.

## HUNDON  TL 739488

South Porch: Chequer base.

## HUNTINGFIELD  TM 336744

Tower: 1B parapet with panelling. Panelled buttresses.
South Porch:* Front and buttresses: panelled with small quatrefoil below each panel in the two upper stages of panelling; pointed-top quatrefoils on base. Compare with Halesworth and Blyford.
South Aisle: One course of chequer squares on parapet with panelled pinnacles at south-east and south-west corners.

## IKEN  TM 412567

Tower: 1S parapet with panelling. Panelled buttresses.
South Porch: Panelling on front.

## ILKETSHALL ST ANDREW  TM 379873

Tower: Round tower with two octagonal upper stages. Feigned two-light windows in diagonal faces of belfry stage. Octagonal 1S parapet, panelled.

## IPSWICH, St Clement's  TM 168442

Clerestory: Below the string course, single panels between windows but two between the four more widely-spaced eastern windows, and three in the east end bay. Above the string course, narrower panels are paired under finialled canopy heads, and in the wider east end bays they rest on bands of small quatrefoils. On the north side only, alternate pairs of panels rest on emblems.

## IPSWICH, St Helen's                         TM 172445

| | |
|---|---|
| South Porch: | Panelled base. |
| Nave: | Panelled base on south side. |

## IPSWICH, St Lawrence's (XII)                TM 164446

| | |
|---|---|
| Tower:* | Five-stage tower. Walls of the three lower stages are of mixed knapped flint, limestone rubble and erratics, and have angle buttresses faced with vertical chequer. Panelling on plinth. Chequer panel each side of west door at arch level. The upper two stages, rebuilt in 1882, are ashlar stone with flushwork decoration filling the whole wall space: the fourth stage has diagonal chequer above a band of panels, and the belfry stage has three stages of panelling interrupted by a circular motif each side of the belfry openings, chequer above the belfry opening arches, and a frieze of wheel motifs below the openwork parapet. |
| Nave: | Panelling on plinth. |
| Chancel: | Inscription in Gothic script below east window. Three emblems each side of window, flushwork and relief. |

## IPSWICH, St Margaret's                      TM 166448

| | |
|---|---|
| Tower: | 2B parapet, panelling and quatrefoils in top stage, and lozenges and panelling in frieze. |
| South Porch: | Panelling on front and buttresses, and on base and parapet only on side walls. |
| South Aisle:* | Large three-light intersected tracery feigned window with knapped flint infilling in rubble-flint west wall. Panelling and emblems in parapet. |
| South Transept: | Band of pommée crosses on parapet. |
| North Transept: | Emblems on buttresses but most flint lost. |

## IPSWICH, St Mary-le-Quay                    TM 165441

| | |
|---|---|
| Tower: | Panelled base and band of shields above west door. |

## IPSWICH, St Mary Stoke                      TM 163438

| | |
|---|---|
| South Porch: | Panelling on front with large chequer in gable. |

Chancel: Large chequer on east end gable.
South Transept: Large chequer on gable.

## IPSWICH, St Mary-le-Tower     TM 164447

Tower: Top stage chequer with bands of panelling below belfry openings, over south door and corresponding levels on east and west.
Clerestory: Chequer above string course.
Nave: On west end, a band of panelling between doorway and large west window.

## IPSWICH, St Matthew's     TM 158448

Tower: 2B parapet with frieze of panelling below openwork top.
South Aisle: Single panels in merlons; between, alternating with short bands of cresting, crowned initial I each side of a blank shield in a circle (c.f. Coltishall). Buttresses have panelling on face and base.

## IPSWICH, St Nicholas'     TM 163448

Tower: 2S parapet. Narrow panels in upper stage, some with cross or shields inset, some with quatrefoil below; emblems in frieze. Panelled base and buttresses. Ornate cross and two narrow panels between twin belfry openings. Band of panels and relief emblems above west door.

plate 70. Kedington. Flush knapped flint panels on the 14th-century tower, a primitive flushwork precursor.

Flint Flushwork

## IPSWICH, St Peter's  TM 164441

Tower;  2S parapet with panelling in upper stage and panelling and emblems in frieze.

Gateways:  Gateposts of south and west entrances from street into churchyard have crowned flushwork initials.

## IPSWICH, St Stephen's  TM 164445

Tower:  Some panelling on base.

## IXWORTH  TL 932704

Tower:  2S parapet with panelling and emblems in upper stage and emblems in frieze. Emblems on base and buttresses.

South Porch:  Panelled front. Chequer base and panelled parapet on side wall.

## IXWORTH THORPE (VI)  TL 917725

South Porch:  Brick. Brick flushwork panels on buttresses and in side wall parapets.

## KEDINGTON (70)  TL 705470

Tower:  On the belfry stage, pairs of knapped flint panels are set flush within rubble flint walling, their edges making straight joints between the two materials. The panel heads are crudely trefoiled in stone or mortar and the separating mullions are mainly brick patching. This is a primitive form of flush decoration, though not true flushwork as it lacks ashlar stone.

## KELSALE  TM 388652

Tower:*  1B parapet with panelling in merlons and elaborated quatrefoil flanked by panels below indents, cf. Yoxford.

South Porch:*  Panelling dado on front. Panelled battlemented parapet with cross keys emblem in apex. Vertical chequer and single panel on face of buttresses.

## KENTON  TM 192659

Tower:  Shallow 1B parapet mainly brick with a few flints. Each face has four flushwork roundels comprising inner circle and outer ring in stone with knapped flint between, joined by a single stone strip.

plate 71. Kersey. A variety of flushwork themes on the south porch

## KERSEY (IX) (71)  TM 003439

| | |
|---|---|
| Tower:* | 1B parapet, cinquefoil-headed panels in the merlons and below the indents each contain a finialled quatrefoil. Four panels each side of west window. Three-light windows in the third stage have their centre lights infilled flush with knapped flint. The base has three stages of single chequer squares separated by stone string courses. |
| Porch South:* | Base of three stages: panelling, quatrefoils and diagonal chequer. Panelled front, the top stage terminating with curious bi-foiled heads. Shallow pitch battlemented parapet with diagonal chequer. Side walls have the same base and parapet patterns as the front. Panelled buttresses have similar bases. |
| North Porch: | Three-stage base as tower, on front, sides and buttresses. |
| North Aisle: | Three-stage base as tower, and chequer parapet. |

## KESSINGLAND  TM 528862

| | |
|---|---|
| Tower: | Panelling on base. Panelling on buttresses changes abruptly to staggered vertical chequer about halfway up the tower's second stage |

## KETTLEBURGH  TM 265606

| | |
|---|---|
| Tower: | 1S parapet with panelling. Panelled base and buttresses. |
| South Porch: | Panelled base on front and side walls. |

## KNODISHALL  TM 426619

| | |
|---|---|
| Tower: | Level parapet, panelled, in poor condition. Emblems on buttresses. |

## LAVENHAM  TL 913490

| | |
|---|---|
| Tower: | Five-pointed star of the de Vere family inset within the four walls. |
| Clerestories: | Inset shields and five-pointed stars alternate in the spandrels between the window arches. |
| South Chapel: | Panelled dado; paired panels with canopy heads on walls correspond with window heights. |
| North Chapel: | Wall flushwork similar to South Chapel; battlemented parapet has panelling in the merlons and blank shields surrounded by quatrefoils below the indents. |
| East Chapel: | Panelled dado; panelled parapet with small quatrefoil below indents. |

plate 72. Little Waldingfield. Alternating panels of rubble and knapped flint in the tower parapet.

## LAXFIELD     TM 287726

Tower:*     Four-stage tower of similar design to Redenhall and Eye, but built of squared rubble stone, not flint. The west front is entirely faced with bands of flushwork panelling, some of the bands being of half-width panels. There is a square of chequerwork below the small window in the second stage. Only the belfry stages of the south, east and north faces have flushwork panelling. Base and polygonal buttresses are panelled.

South Porch:     Panelling on buttresses and on the base of the front.

## LEISTON     TM 438625

Tower:     1S parapet with panelling and emblems. Panelling and chequer on buttresses.

## LETHERINGHAM     TM 269587

Tower:     1S parapet with panelling. Panelling on buttresses.

## LITTLE FAKENHAM     TL 911766

Tower:     Chequer base.

## LITTLE GLEMHAM         TM 346588

Tower: 2B parapet with panelling and emblems in upper stage. Panelled base.

## LITTLE STONHAM         TM 111602

Tower: 2S parapet with panelling and emblems in both stages. Large Marian monogram with smaller letters interposed in central merlon on three faces. Panelled base.
Chancel: Chequer on buttresses. Single emblem on peak of east gable.

## LITTLE THURLOW         TL 680512

Tower:* 1B parapet with chequer of slightly horizontal proportions.

## LITTLE WALDINGFIELD (72)         TL 923452

Tower: Triple-stepped parapet, zoned as 'Norwich' style but without inset motifs. Zones are alternately faced with knapped and rubble flints.

## LONG MELFORD (73)         TL 865468

Tower: Present tower built 1898-1903. 1B parapet with panelling. Emblems alternating with small panels in base. Elegant dado of paired panels below finialled canopy heads, each unit separated by a vertical band of five narrow panels one above the other. Emblem bands below the belfry opening and also lower down.
Clerestory:* The flushwork between each of the closely-spaced windows comprises paired panels under a finialled and crocketted canopy head whose tracery occurs at the level of the window tracery; a division between the upper and lower stages of the panels coincides with the window transome level creating a close affinity between the architecture and the flushwork. Above the window arches inscriptions run between the flushwork finials with blank shields in the spandrel spaces below. The battlemented parapet has panelling in the merlons and emblems below the indents, this pattern being carried across the east gable of the nave. Apart from the inscriptions, these flushwork themes closely match those on the clerestory at Cavendish.
South Aisle: Panelled dado. Crocketted finials above window arches.
Lady Chapel:* Panelled dado; paired two-stage panelling on walls, of

plate 73. Long Melford. Indiscriminate motifs in the gables are poorly related to the panelling below on the east wall of the Lady Chapel.

the same pattern as on the clerestory, with blank shields between the finials. In the three east gables, above a band of panelling, recessed stone squares are arbitrarily surrounded by an assortment of finials, blank shields, panels and bands.

## LOUND  TM 505990

South Porch: Panelled base on front.
Chancel: Panelled buttresses.

## LOWESTOFT  TM 541941

Tower: 1B parapet with two-stage panelling in merlons and four soufflet quatrefoils below indents. In the belfry stage, flushwork arcading below a stone band with small quatrefoils above is interrupted by apparently later belfry openings.

South Porch:* Two-storey. Chequer base on front and sides. Four stages of panelling on front; in the upper stage, the four panels each side of the window are united under arch heads to form feigned windows. Front buttresses have vertical chequer on faces and panelling on the inside returns.

Aisles:* Chequer base. Buttresses have chequer bases and fine

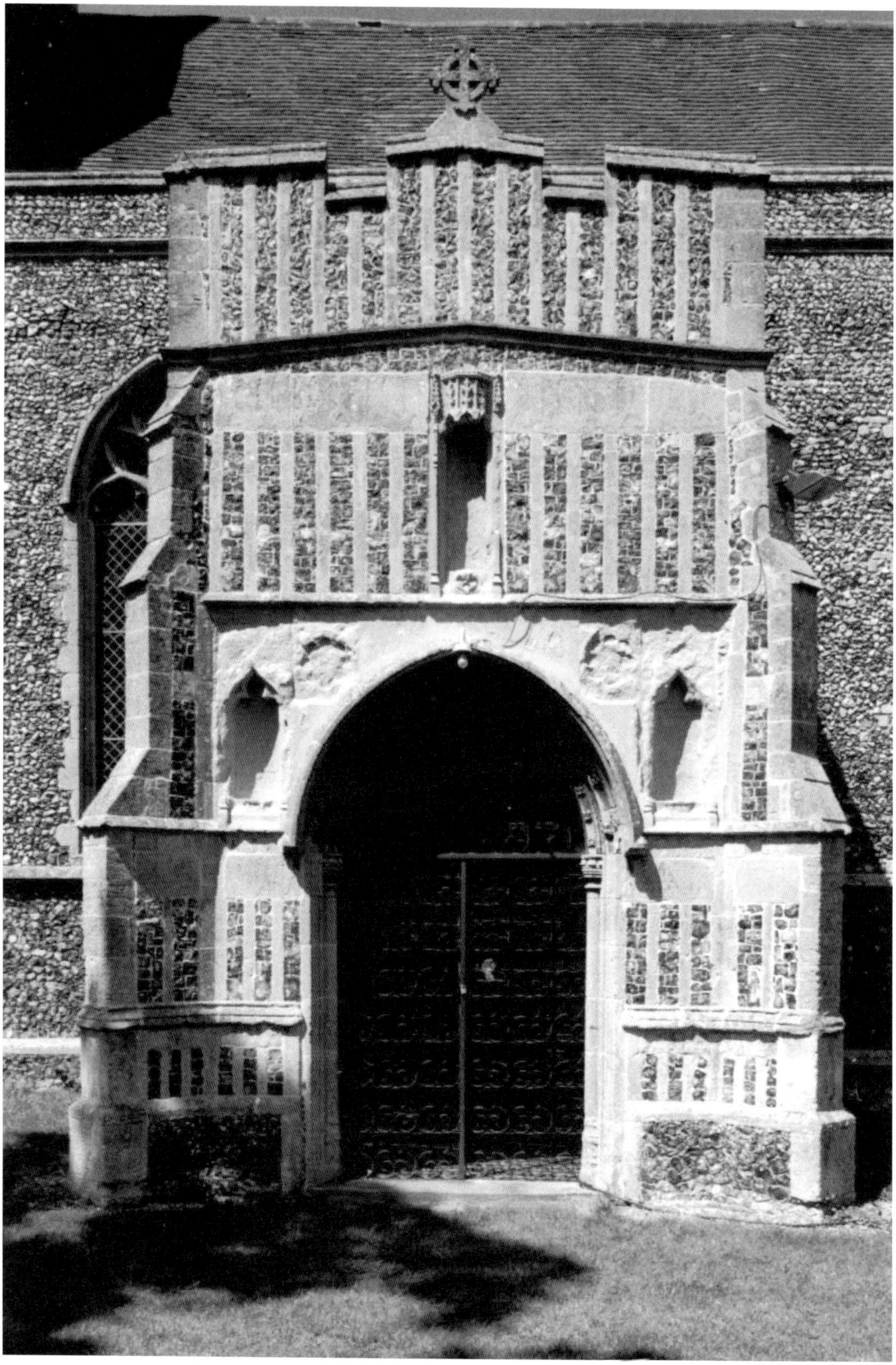

proudwork panelling on south aisle and vertical chequer on north.

Chancel:* Chequer base, and buttresses similar to south aisle.

## MARKET WESTON (74)     TL 991782

South Porch:* Tall, with panelled front and buttresses. All the panels of knapped flint are plain rectangles and except in the parapet, have shallow-sunk stone heads. In the parapet the flints and stone strips between extend right up to the copings.

## MARLESFORD     TM 323583

Tower: 1B parapet with diagonal chequer.
South Porch: Panelling on front.

## MARTLESHAM     TM 262469

Tower: 1S parapet with panelling and emblems. Emblems on base and one above door on west face. Paired panels and emblems on buttresses.

## MELLIS     TM 095743

South Porch: Two-storey. Chequer base on front.
Nave: Chequer on base and buttresses.
Chancel: Panelled dado above panelled base on east end.

## MENDHAM     TM 279829

South Porch: Rectangular panels on front with foliated panels in parapet; rectangular panels on base and parapet of side walls.

## MENDLESHAM     TM 104658

Tower: 2S parapet with panelling in the upper stage and quatrefoils with small panels between in the frieze. Emblems on base. Emblems and panelling on buttresses.
South Porch: Panelling in main stage on front and buttresses. Band of quatrefoils above the arch, and above these, four crowned monograms and Ms. Panelled bases and parapets on front and sides.
North Porch: Two-storey. Panelling on front and on front and side parapets.

plate 74. Plain rectangular panels on the front of Market Weston church porch.

plate 75. Panels with heads of different shapes and a shallow stone relief of four small circles at the top of a porch butress at Metfield church.

## METFIELD (75)  TM 294803

Tower: 1B parapet finished with a cement rendering, leaving small flint panels in merlons only.
South Porch: Two-storey. Panelled front in five stages, some panels having small shallow-sunk trefoils in their stone spandrels; also shallow-sunk stone quatrefoils appear in the buttresses and below the indents of the battlemented parapet. Panelled side parapets.
Nave: Vertical chequer on buttresses with chequer squares on the bases on the north side.

## MIDDLETON  TM 430678

Tower: 1S parapet with panelling and emblems. Chequer and vertical chequer on buttresses.

## MILDENHALL  TL 710746

North Aisle: Chequer on walls.
North Porch: Chequer on base.

## MONEWDEN  TM 239587

Tower: 1S parapet. Panelling in steps and merlons, emblems in indents. Panelled base and buttresses.

## MONKS ELEIGH  TL 966478

Tower: 2B parapet with panelling in upper stage, and panelling and emblems in frieze. Panelling on base and buttresses.

## MONK SOHAM  TM 213651

Tower: 1B parapet with chequer.
South Porch: Panels on front and in base of side walls.

## MUTFORD (42)  TM 486886

Tower:* Round tower with octagonal top. Two-light feigned windows in diagonals of octagon. Octagonal 1B parapet with panelling and emblems.
Chancel:* Finialled panels in dado on east end and on buttresses.

## NEEDHAM MARKET  TM 087552

Buttresses: Emblems on lower stage of the three eastern buttresses of the south wall, on two of which a pair of canopied

| Nave: | panels above. Relief inscriptions at top of buttresses contain no flint infill – were they originally flushwork? A modern west extension has two courses of chequer at eaves level. |

## NEWBOURNE                                           TM 273431

Tower: 1S parapet with panelling.

## NORTH COVE                                          TM 462893

South Porch: The brick gable bears a pattern of separate knapped flint lozenges but the clarity of the design is dimmed by weathering and repairs.

## NORTON                                              TL 962663

South Porch: Chequer base and parapet on front and side walls. Chequer base on buttresses.
Aisles: Chequer parapets. Chequer base on south aisle.

## OAKLEY                                              TM 157774

Tower: 1B parapet with panelling.
South Porch: Two-storey with panelled front and buttresses, and panelling on bases and parapets of side walls.

## OCCOLD                                              TM 156709

Tower: 1S parapet with panelling. Panelled base and buttresses.

## OFFTON                                              TM 066497

Tower: 1S parapet with panelling.

## OLD NEWTON                                          TM 059625

Tower: 1B parapet with panelling.

## PALGRAVE                                            TM 115785

South Porch:* Two-storey. Panelled front and buttresses and a band of quatrefoils above the arch. Stepped parapets on front and sides have panelling and relief emblems.
North Porch: Panelling on buttresses.
Aisles: Panelling on buttresses.

## PARHAM                                         TM 309606

| | |
|---|---|
| Tower: | Rectangular panels on base. Vertical chequer on buttresses. |
| North Porch: | Emblems on base of front and sides. Panelling on front and buttresses. |
| Nave: | Vertical chequer on buttresses. |
| Chancel: | Square chequer on base of buttresses. |

## PEASENHALL                                     TM 355692

| | |
|---|---|
| Tower: | 1S parapet with panelling and emblems. Panelled bases on buttresses. |
| North Porch: | Panelling on front and buttresses. |

## PETTAUGH                                       TM 168597

| | |
|---|---|
| Tower: | 1S parapet with panelling. |

## PETTISTREE                                     TM 298550

| | |
|---|---|
| Tower: | 2B parapet with chequer in both stages, but larger squares in frieze. Chequer base, diagonal on west, straight on north and south. Vertical chequer on buttresses. |
| Nave: | Chequer base on south and on buttresses. |

## PRESTON ST MARY                                TL 946503

| | |
|---|---|
| Tower: | Chequer base. |
| North Porch:* | Base, walls and parapets on front and sides, and angle buttresses all fully panelled. |

## RATTLESDEN (41)                                TL 978591

| | |
|---|---|
| Clerestory:* | Battlemented south parapet with pairs of canopied or supermullioned panels in alternate merlons and a variety of different emblems below the indents, mainly symbols of the apostles. |

## REDGRAVE                                       TM 058783

| | |
|---|---|
| South Clerestory: | Emblems between windows, in poor condition. |

## RENDHAM                                        TM 350645

| | |
|---|---|
| Tower: | 1B parapet with panelling. Panelling on buttresses. Two panels below west window, as at Swefling. |
| North Porch: | Panelling on buttresses. |

## RENDLESHAM	TM 325528

Tower:	1B parapet with diagonal chequer. Square chequer base and vertical chequer on buttresses.

## REYDON	TM 491782

Tower:	1B parapet with panelling.

## RICKINGHALL INFERIOR	TM 039752

Tower:	Round tower with octagonal upper stage and panelled 1B parapet.
South Porch:	Two-storey. Band of emblems above arch flanked by pairs of panels. All emblem flintwork lost.

## RICKINGHALL SUPERIOR	TM 041746

Tower:	1S parapet with panelling and emblems.
South Porch:*	Two-storey. Over the arch, a band of six crowned sacred monograms.
Nave:	Proudwork panelled base and dado course of flushwork blank shields.

## RINGSFIELD	TM 403884

Tower:	1S parapet with brick quoins and copings, with two stages of staggered brick flushwork panelling.

## RISHANGLES	TM 160687

Tower:	1S parapet with panelling. Panelled base.

## ROUGHAM	TL 912626

Tower:*	2S parapet. Emblems below indents and mainly panelling in merlons and steppings, except that the central merlons each have different motifs, e.g. on the south a five-line Gothic inscription, and on the east above a pair of plain shields a large crowned Marian monogram superimposed with two lily-in-vase motifs. In the frieze, an undulating strand weaves under and over encircled and raindrop shapes in the intervening spaces. Panelling and emblems on buttresses.

## RUSHMERE ST ANDREW	TM 196461

Tower:	1S parapet with panelling.

## SANTON DOWNHAM                                        TL 816877

    Tower:          Panelling, emblems and inscriptions in base but much flint lost.

## SAXMUNDHAM                                             TM 389630

    Tower:          1S parapet with panelling.
    South
      Clerestory:   Panels in groups of three between windows above and below the string course; most flint missing but remnants around the two west windows.

## SAXTEAD                                                TM 263658

    South Porch:   Panelling on front and on base of side walls.

## SIBTON                                                 TM 368695

    Tower:          1B parapet faced with flint cobbles; three inset flushwork motifs in each face comprising, centrally, a pair of knapped flint panels within a stone rectangle, flanked by knapped flint lozenges framed with stone. A similar arrangement to Benacre but with different motifs.

## SNAPE                                                  TM 395594

    Tower:          1S parapet with panelling and emblems. Emblems and vertical chequer on buttresses.
    South Porch:   Panelled front with quatrefoil base.

## SOUTH COVE                                             TM 500809

    Tower:          1S parapet with panelling and emblems. Panelled buttresses.

## SOUTH ELMHAM ALL SAINTS                                TM 330828

    South Porch:   Chequer on front wall between plinth and arch springer level.

## SOUTH ELMHAM ST CROSS                                  TM 299843

    Tower:*         1B parapet with panelling in merlons and pretty tracery motifs below indents. Chequer on buttresses.

## SOUTH ELMHAM ST MARGARET                               TM 350853

    Tower:          Panelling on base.

plate 76. Southwold. Crowned Lombardic lettering around the arch of the tower west window.

## SOUTH ELMHAM ST MICHAEL            TM 341840

Tower:            1S parapet with panelling and emblems in merlons and steppings. Relief emblems below indents.

## SOUTH ELMHAM ST PETER            TM 337849

Tower:            1B parapet with panelling. Chequer on buttresses.

## SOUTH ELMHAM ST PETER, St Peter's Hall            TM 336854

North Wall
and Porch:            Emblems in plinth, but most flint infill now missing.

## SOUTHOLT (8)            TM 193689

South Porch:*            The whole front above the base is a chequer of 4-inch squares, each flint square trimmed from a single flint, those in the gable white.

Nave:            Panelling on base and buttresses of west end.

## SOUTHWOLD (I) (76)            TM 507764

Tower:*            Single-stage level parapet with quatrefoils. Panelled base and buttresses. Panelling each side of west door and west window. An inscription in crowned Lombardic letters following the curve of the west window arch reads: SCT EDMUND ORA P NOBIS. Above this, a large panel of chequer.

South Porch:*            Two-storey. The front has a base of M initials and monograms; proudwork panels each side of the archway extend to its full height and contain intermediate subdivisions in flush stonework, so creating flushwork within proudwork. A band of upright and inverted trowel-shaped emblems above the arch forms the base of the upper stage which has flushwork panelling. The buttresses have similar base to the front and are panelled with proudwork. Chequer patterned side walls have a base of panelling. Panelling and emblems on the battlemented parapets of the side walls are direct interpretations in flushwork of the same motifs in relief on the front parapet. Vertical chequer on stair turret.

Chancel:            Panelled base and buttresses. Dado of panelling across east wall.

Aisles:            Panelled base and vertical chequer on buttresses.

## STOWLANGTOFT            TL 957682

Tower:            Single-stage level parapet with chequer. Straight and

| | diagonal chequer base. |
|---|---|
| South Porch:* | Chequer front with diagonal chequer base. Diagonal chequer buttresses. Chequer base on side walls. Level panelled parapets on front and side walls. |
| Nave and Chancel:* | Continuous chequer base including buttresses, some straight, some diagonal. Level parapet with three courses of straight chequer. Vertical chequer on buttresses. |

## STOWMARKET                           TM 049587

| | |
|---|---|
| Tower: | 1B parapet, panelled. |
| South Porch: | Tall single-storey. Three-course chequer base on front and side walls. Panelling and diagonal chequer on front wall. |
| North Porch: | Front and buttresses panelled. |

## STRADBROKE                           TM 232740

| | |
|---|---|
| Tower: | 1B parapet with panelling. |
| South Porch: | Panelling on buttresses. |
| North Porch: | Panelled parapet on front and sides. |

## STRATFORD ST ANDREW                  TM 358601

| | |
|---|---|
| Tower: | 1S parapet with panelling and emblems. Panelling on buttresses. |

## STRATFORD ST MARY (27)               TM 052346

| | |
|---|---|
| Tower: | 1B parapet with panelling in merlons and quatrefoils below indents. Short inscriptions each side of belfry openings, one showing a date of 1878. |
| Clerestories: | Panels between windows. Battlemented parapet with panelling. |
| North Aisle and Chancel Chapel:* | Inscription in Gothic script on the plinth of the east wall and continued across the buttresses and along the north and west walls. Panelling, emblems and letters of the alphabet on the buttresses. Letters also on wall. Battlemented parapet with panels containing emblems, returned on east and west ends. |
| North Porch: | Tall panels each side of arch on all faces. Parapet as north aisle. |
| South Aisle: | Battlemented parapet with panels in merlons and quatrefoils and semi-quatrefoils between, returned on east end. Panelling on one buttress. |

## SUDBOURNE                                       TM 421519

Tower: 1B parapet with relief flushwork: panelling in merlons and below indents is infilled with flint cobbles.

## SUDBURY, All Saints                             TL 869410

Tower: Panels on buttresses.
Chancel Aisle: Two-course chequer plinth on south and east.

## SUDBURY, St Gregory's                           TL 871415

North Aisle: Four-course chequer dado.

## SUDBURY, St Peter's                             TL 875413

Aisles: Two-course chequer base on north. Quatrefoil emblem base on south.
South Porch: Quatrefoil emblem base.

## SWEFLING                                        TM 347638

Tower: Level parapet with emblems and panelling. Panelling on buttresses. Two panels below west window, as at Rendham.
South Porch: Panelled base and front. Emblems on front and side parapets.

## TANNINGTON                                      TM 242675

Tower: Chequer base.
South Porch: Panelling on front and on side parapets.

## THEBERTON (4)                                   TM 438659

Tower: Round tower with octagonal upper stage; feigned two-light windows in the diagonal faces replicating the Y-tracery of the belfry openings. 1B parapet with panelling and emblems.
South Porch: Built up against the west wall of the south aisle. Unusual repeated emblems (a quatrefoil with pointed top lobe and wavy strips in the top corners) form the base on the front, west wall and buttresses, and are comparable to those in the tower base at Thrandeston. Panelling on front and buttresses. Flints from the west wall parapet flushwork are all missing but the pattern can be seen to be an interpretation in the flat of the relief wavy tracery of the front parapet, as at Ufford.
South Aisle: Emblems on buttresses.

## THORNDON                                    TM 142697

Buttresses: Proudwork panelling on faces of chancel buttresses flanking priest's door and at south-west and north-west of nave. Flushwork chequer plinths, some with unusual variations.

## THORNHAM MAGNA                              TM 104714

South Porch: Shallow-sunk stone head panelling on front. Panelled base.

## THRANDESTON (52)                            TM 117765

Tower: Base course of repeated identical emblems: each comprises a quatrefoil with pointed top lobe on which is superimposed a lozenge containing a smaller quatrefoil, with wavy strips in the upper corners, as on Theberton porch. These appear on each face of the diagonal buttresses, and ten times on each side of the tower. Above these, on the west face, a dado band of seven identical larger emblems – blank shields on a geometric background. Panelled buttresses.

## TOSTOCK                                     TL 960637

Tower: Panels on face of buttresses.
Nave: Emblems on buttress plinths.

## TROSTON                                     TL 900723

South Porch:* Panelled front. Panelling and emblems in front parapet and emblems in side parapets.

## TUDDENHAM (near Ipswich)                    TM 192485

Tower: 1B parapet with panelling. Panelling on buttresses.

## TUNSTALL                                    TM 363552

Tower: Panelled base.
South Porch: Panelling on front and buttresses.

## UFFORD (28)                                 TM 299522

Tower: Square-panelled base and vertical chequer on buttresses.
South Porch:* Repeated blank shields on eight-pointed star backgrounds occupy the bases of the front and side walls

plate 77. Walsham le Willows. Diagonal chequer on the front and buttresses of the north porch.

with other motifs on the bases of the buttresses. Front, west side and buttresses are panelled. Side wall parapets are flushwork interpretations of the relief wavy tracery of the front parapet (cf. Blyford and Theberton).

## WALBERSWICK                                                     TM 490748

| | |
|---|---|
| Tower: | 2S parapet with panelling on upper stage, the frieze in relief stone. Panelled base and buttresses. |
| South Porch: | Two-storey. Panelling on front and buttresses. |
| South Aisle:* | Panelling on buttresses. Diagonal chequer parapet with |

alternate bays of normal-sized and small squares. Below the window in the rebuilt east wall, a shallow band of decorative panels, mainly small chequer variations randomly embodying exquisitely cut miniature emblems.

## WALSHAM LE WILLOWS (77)     TM 000712

| | |
|---|---|
| Tower: | 1B parapet with panelling. |
| North Porch:* | Diagonal chequer on the front, the buttresses and the base of the side walls. On the face of the buttresses, the chequer squares are smaller. |
| Clerestory:* | Below the string course, single emblems between the closely-spaced windows, and three at each end. |
| Aisles: | Diagonal chequer base and vertical chequer on buttresses. |

## WANGFORD     TM 466792

| | |
|---|---|
| Tower: | 2S parapet with panelling in merlons and steppings and emblems below indents. Plain walling in frieze. Panelling on face of buttresses. |
| Chancel: | Band of small panels and three large quatrefoils below east window (1878). Panelling on buttress bases. |
| N. Aisle and S. Vestry: | Panelling on buttress bases. |

## WATTISFIELD     TM 010742

| | |
|---|---|
| Tower: | Panelled base. |
| South Porch: | Minor emblem decoration on front and buttresses. |

## WATTISHAM     TM 010513

| | |
|---|---|
| Tower: | 1S parapet with panelling. |

## WENHASTON     TM 425755

| | |
|---|---|
| Tower: | Single-stage parapet with raised corners, panelled. Panelled buttresses. |

## WESTERFIELD     TM 175476

| | |
|---|---|
| Tower: | 1B parapet with panelling. Panelled buttresses. |

## WESTHALL     TM 423805

| | |
|---|---|
| Tower: | 1B parapet with panelling. Feigned window above a Greek cross on lower stage of buttresses. |
| North Porch: | Panelled base on front. |

## WETHERDEN  TM 009628

South Aisle: Emblems and panelling on base and emblems on buttresses, including lily-in-vase, but virtually all flint lost.

## WETHERINGSETT  TM 128669

Tower: Wide angle buttresses with three-square width of chequer on all stages. Two-square chequer base.
South Porch: Single-course chequer base on front. Vertical chequer on diagonal buttresses. Panelling on parapet.
Clerestory: Single panel at east end, both sides.
Aisles: Chequer course on base of north-side buttresses. Greek crosses in face of buttresses.

## WEYBREAD  TM 241801

Tower: Round tower. Between the belfry openings, lancet-type feigned windows of knapped flint framed by brickwork flush with the wall face.
South Porch:* Panelled gabled front and buttresses. Panelling on base of side walls.

## WICKHAM MARKET  TM 302558

Tower: Octagonal. 1B parapet with diagonal chequer. Proudwork replicas of belfry openings in diagonal faces of octagon. One course of chequer squares on base.
Nave: One course of chequer squares on base of west wall and west buttresses.

## WICKHAM SKEITH  TM 099693

Tower: Chequer on buttresses with chequer cross motif on base.
South Porch: Two-storey. Panelling on front up to arch level only.
North Porch: Panelling on front; emblems and panels on parapet. Above the arch, a band of square stone panels each bearing a shallow-sunk impression of a crowned M, comparable to Appendix C instances but not flushwork.
Nave: Vertical chequer on buttresses.

## WILBY  TM 241721

Tower: 1S parapet with north face simply subdivided into nine rectangular zones in the manner of the 'Norwich' style. Some zones on the west, south and east faces are

|  |  |
|---|---|
| | foliated, but each slightly differently; blank shields above a band of four diagonal chequer squares appear below the indents on the west and south faces. Panelled base and buttresses. Band of quatrefoils above the west door. |
| South Porch: | Emblems on base of side walls. |
| Clerestory: | Two-light feigned windows between the clerestory windows are the same height but their tracery differs and their jambs and mullions are traversed by the string course. |

## WINGFIELD, St Andrew     TM 230769

Aisles and
  Chancel:    Single course of alernating stone and flint squares in plinth.

## WINGFIELD Castle     TM 222772

Gatehouse:    Panelled base on turrets.

## WITNESHAM     TM 180509

Tower:    1B parapet with panelling.

## WOODBRIDGE (10)     TM 271491

Tower:*    2B parapet. Panelling surmounted by small emblems in merlons and emblems below indents. The frieze comprises alternately upright and inverted hexafoil triangles forming a running wavy pattern between bands of single diagonal chequer squares. Emblems on base, and panelling and emblems alongside and above west door.

North Porch:*    Front panelled. Side walls panelled in three stages with a band of emblems above. Polygonal buttresses also panelled. Emblems on base of side walls and buttresses. Stepped parapets on front and side walls have panelling in merlons and steppings, and emblems below indents.

Clerestory:    Simple panelling below string course.

North Aisle:    Proudwork base. Panelling on east wall parapet and above north entrance at east end.

## WOOLPIT (XIII)     TL 974625

South Porch:    Big. Chequer on east side wall only.

Clerestory:*    A string course bisects the spaces between windows and between each window below the string course, two small panels flanking a central emblem rest on a pair of

|  | larger cinquefoil panels; above, a rectangle of chequer forms the base of another pair of panels that have finely traceried heads. The same design appears on both sides, and unquestionably this must be the most spectacular of all flushwork clerestories. |
|---|---|
| Chancel: | Chequer parapet. |

## WOOLVERSTONE — TM 190386

| Tower: | 1B parapet with two-tier panelling in merlons and quatrefoils in indents. Panelling on buttresses. |
|---|---|
| Chancel: | A single row of panels across full width of east wall beneath the east window. |

plate 78. Supermullioned panels in the parapet, canopied panels and an unusually varied display of motifs on the front and buttresses of Worlingworth church porch.

156  *Flint Flushwork*

## WORLINGHAM  TM 445899

Tower: 1S parapet with panelling.
North Porch: Panelling on buttresses.

## WORLINGWORTH (78)  TM 234688

Tower: 1B parapet with panels in merlons only. Chequer on buttresses.
South Porch: Panelling and emblems on front and buttresses, and also on base and parapets of side walls.
Nave: On the base, panels in pairs alternate with emblems of interesting variety, but much of the flint is missing.

## WORTHAM (39)  TM 084788

Clerestory: The string course is located level with the bottom of the window tracery, about eighteen inches below the arch springing. The window arches have red brick voussoirs alternating with flint and these are continued down the jambs to the string course, below which, between each window, two emblems side by side rest on plain rectangular panels.
Chancel: Vertical chequer on buttresses.

## WRENTHAM  TM 489830

Tower: 2B parapet with panelling and emblems in the upper

|  | stage and panelling in the frieze. Emblems in base. |
|---|---|
| South Porch: | Panelling on front and chequer parapets on front and sides. |

### WYVERSTONE      TM 042679

| Tower: | 1B parapet, chequer. Square chequer on plinths of buttresses and vertical chequer on faces. |
|---|---|
| Chancel: | Chequer plinths on buttresses. |

### YAXLEY      TM 121739

| Tower: | Chequer on base of buttresses. |
|---|---|
| North Porch: | Two-storey. On the front, small emblems above a panelled base, panels both sides of niches each side of the arch and on buttresses; above the arch a band of fourteen small crowned Ms. A single panel each side of the two windows of the upper stage. Three courses of chequer on the base of the west wall. |

### YOXFORD      TM 394690

| Tower: | 1B parapet; panelling in merlons, and elaborated quatrefoil flanked by panels below the indents, cf. Kelsale. |
|---|---|

# ESSEX

### ALTHORNE (34)      TQ 909989

| Tower: | Crag and knapped flint. Parapet type 1B with diagonal trellis pattern, comparable to the east wall at Barsham. |
|---|---|

### ARDLEIGH (79)      TM 054296

| Tower: | Puddingstone. 1B parapet with brick flushwork. Ordinary flushwork panelling on base. |
|---|---|
| South Porch:* | Panelling on front and buttresses, with quatrefoils also on battlemented parapet. Panelling on base and parapets of side walls. |

### BARLING      TQ 932897

| Tower: | Stone. A horizontal band of knapped flint about halfway up the tower on all sides; below this on west side, four courses of chequer. |
|---|---|

plate 79. Ardleigh. Victorian brick flushwork panelling in the tower parapet.

## BRIGHTLINGSEA (80)  TM 077188

| | |
|---|---|
| Tower: | 2B parapet. Quatrefoils below indents. Relief frieze. Panelled base on north and south. |
| South Porch: | Panelled base. |
| South Vestry: | Alternating quatrefoils and panels on base; panels in merlons and quatrefoils below indents on parapet, and panelling on buttresses. |
| North Aisle: | On east end only, similar flushwork to south vestry. |

## BULMER  TL 843402

| | |
|---|---|
| Tower: | Two courses of chequer on base. |

## CANEWDON  TQ 896945

| | |
|---|---|
| Tower: | Stone. 1B parapet. Chequer with rough stonework; Greek cross in merlons. |
| South Porch: | Chequer parapet on front and sides; stone cross divides merlons into four flint squares. |

## CHELMSFORD CATHEDRAL (XV)  TL 710069

| | |
|---|---|
| Tower: | 1S parapet with panelling and emblems. |
| South Porch:* | Two-storey. Panelled base and parapet on front, sides and buttresses. Panelling on front. Diagonal chequer on lower half of side walls above which panelling with paired finialled crocketted canopy heads; between these and the parapet, a band of alternating squares of diapered brickwork and flushwork emblems. |
| South Aisle: | Panelled battlemented parapet. |
| Chancel: | Two eastern bays of parapet chequer. Dado and gable on east end chequer. |
| North Transept: | Chequer parapet on shallow gable. |

## CHRISHALL  TL 451387

| | |
|---|---|
| Tower: | 1B parapet with chequer. |

## COLCHESTER, All Saints  TM 998253

| | |
|---|---|
| Tower: | 1B parapet with panelling. Chequer base. |
| North Aisle: | Panelled parapet. |

## COLCHESTER, St John's Abbey Gatehouse  TM 998248

| | |
|---|---|
| North Front: | Panelling in three stages, the taller upper stage comprising panels in pairs under finialled and crocketted canopy heads with lily-in-vase motifs between the finials. |

plate 80. Detail of flushwork panelling from Brightlingsea church.

|  | Polygonal corner turrets have corresponding panelling and a fourth stage at parapet level. The battlemented parapet is panelled and the panel in the central merlon has a lily-in-vase. |
|---|---|
| Other Sides: | Panelled battlemented parapets on south front and side walls. |

## DEDHAM  TM 057332

| Tower: | 1B parapet with panelling. Emblems on base. |
|---|---|
| South Porch: | Two-storey. Panelled base on front and sides. |

| | |
|---|---|
| North Porch: | Two-storey. Panelled base and parapet on front and sides. Panelled buttresses. |
| Aisles: | Panelled base. |

## EARLS COLNE            TL 861289

| | |
|---|---|
| Tower: | 1S parapet with the de Vere arms in relief in the centre merlon and steppings on east and west; remainder panelling, with most panels containing an inset five-pointed star. Polygonal stair turret on south-east corner with knapped flint parapet in three stages, each facet containing an inset star. |

## EAST MERSEA            TM 051142

| | |
|---|---|
| Tower: | Plain rectangular panelling on base. |

## FEERING            TL 872204

| | |
|---|---|
| S. Porch and S. Aisle: | Brick flushwork base. |

## FINGRINGHOE            TM 029204

| | |
|---|---|
| Tower: | Chequer base, the stonework not ashlar, probably crag. |
| South Porch: | Panelled base on front. Chequer parapets. |

## GOLDHANGER            TL 904089

| | |
|---|---|
| Tower: | Crag. A rectangle of chequer, three x eleven squares, above west window. |

## GREAT BROMLEY (81)            TM 083263

| | |
|---|---|
| South Porch:* | Panelled base on front and sides. On the front, including the front splays of the buttresses and the parapet, panels are paired under finialled and crocketted canopy heads and the interposing mullions are extended upwards as finials. The side parapets are panelled, and the front panels on both stages of the buttresses are proudwork. A string course divides the panelling into two stages: the lower stage has simple panels and the upper is similar to the porch front but with single panels between the closely-spaced windows. The battlemented parapet has panelling in the merlons and small panels over quatrefoils below the indents. |
| Clerestory: | |
| South Aisle: | Panelling on base. |

plate 81. Paired panels under canopy heads on Great Bromley church porch. Some of the knapped flint is missing from the front parapet. Proudwork on face of buttresses.

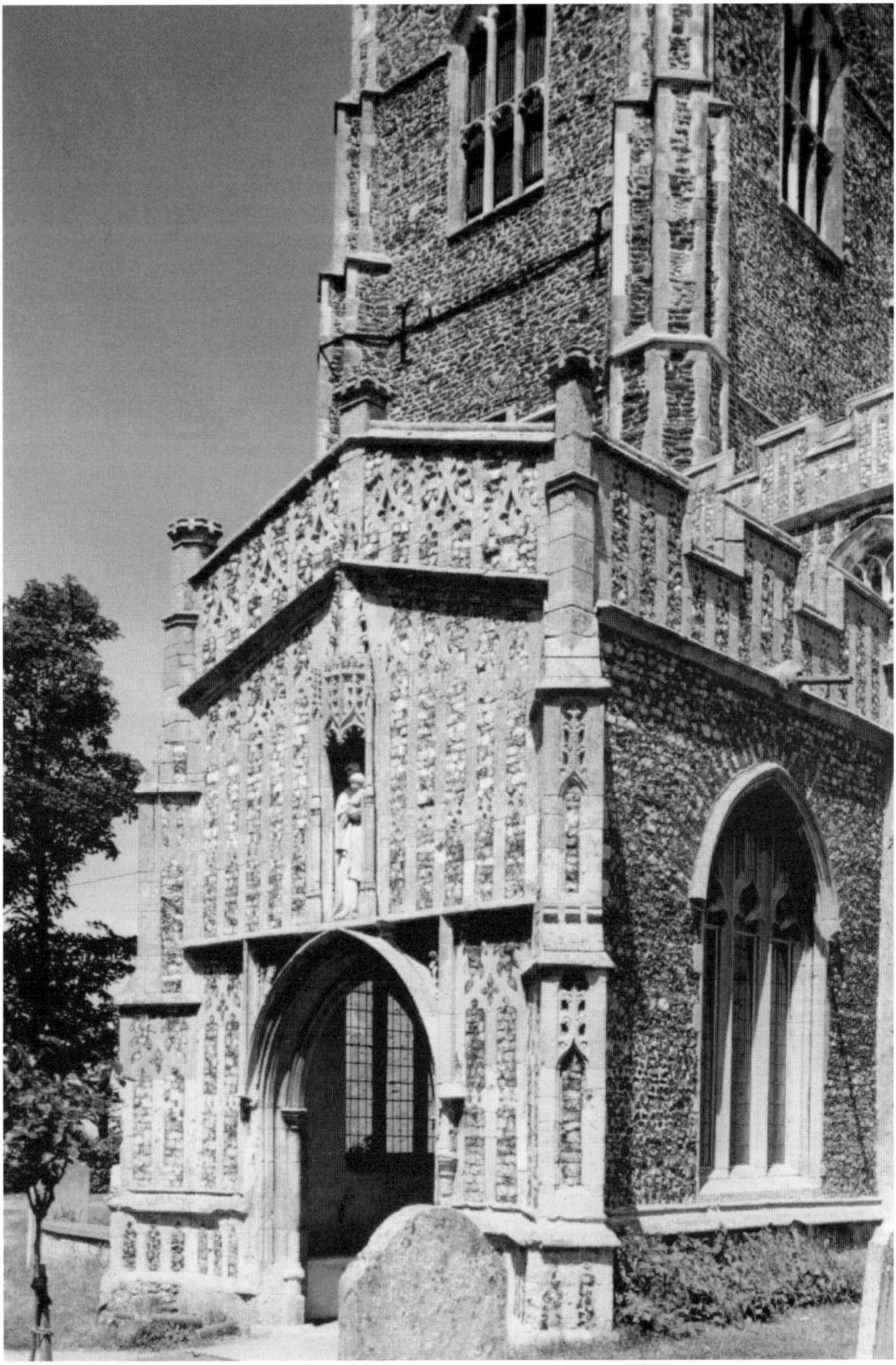

## HADSTOCK                                                     TL 559448

Tower:               Chequer on base and base of buttresses.
South Porch:     Chequer base on front.
Chancel:           Larger chequer on upper parts of south and east walls.
North Vestry:    Larger chequer on upper parts.

## HALSTEAD                                                TL 816307

Tower:               1B parapet with panelling and emblems.

## HIGH EASTER                                      TL 620148

Tower:               Chequer on base and base of buttresses.

## HYTHE, Colchester                          TM 013248

Tower:               2S parapet with panelling and emblems in upper stage and quatrefoils in frieze.

## KIRBY LE SOKEN                         TM 219220

Tower:               1B parapet with chequer.

## LAWFORD (X) (82)                         TM 089316

Tower:*            Original fabric a mixture of puddingstone, septaria and flint but extensively rebuilt in brickwork. The base has remnants of flushwork chequer and in the lower part of the tower, there are remnants of flushwork panelling in two stages in which the stone members are puddingstone. On the stair turret, knapped flint panels in the shape of two superimposed Ts form a pattern within puddingstone.
Chancel:*         Below the windows, in one bay, horizontal bands of knapped flint alternate with brick, and in the other and on the east end there is a chequer of brick and knapped flint.

## LITTLE WAKERING                    TQ 934884

Tower:               Stone. 1B parapet with chequer.

## PURLEIGH                                       TL 842020

Tower:               Stone and knapped flint in alternating bands. Two-course ribbons of chequer on dado and halfway up the tower, but the stonework squares are not ashlar.

plate 82. Remnant of a flushwork pattern on the much-repaired tower of Lawford church. The knapped flint panels are defined by dark puddingstone but the side members of the lower panel have been replaced with brick.

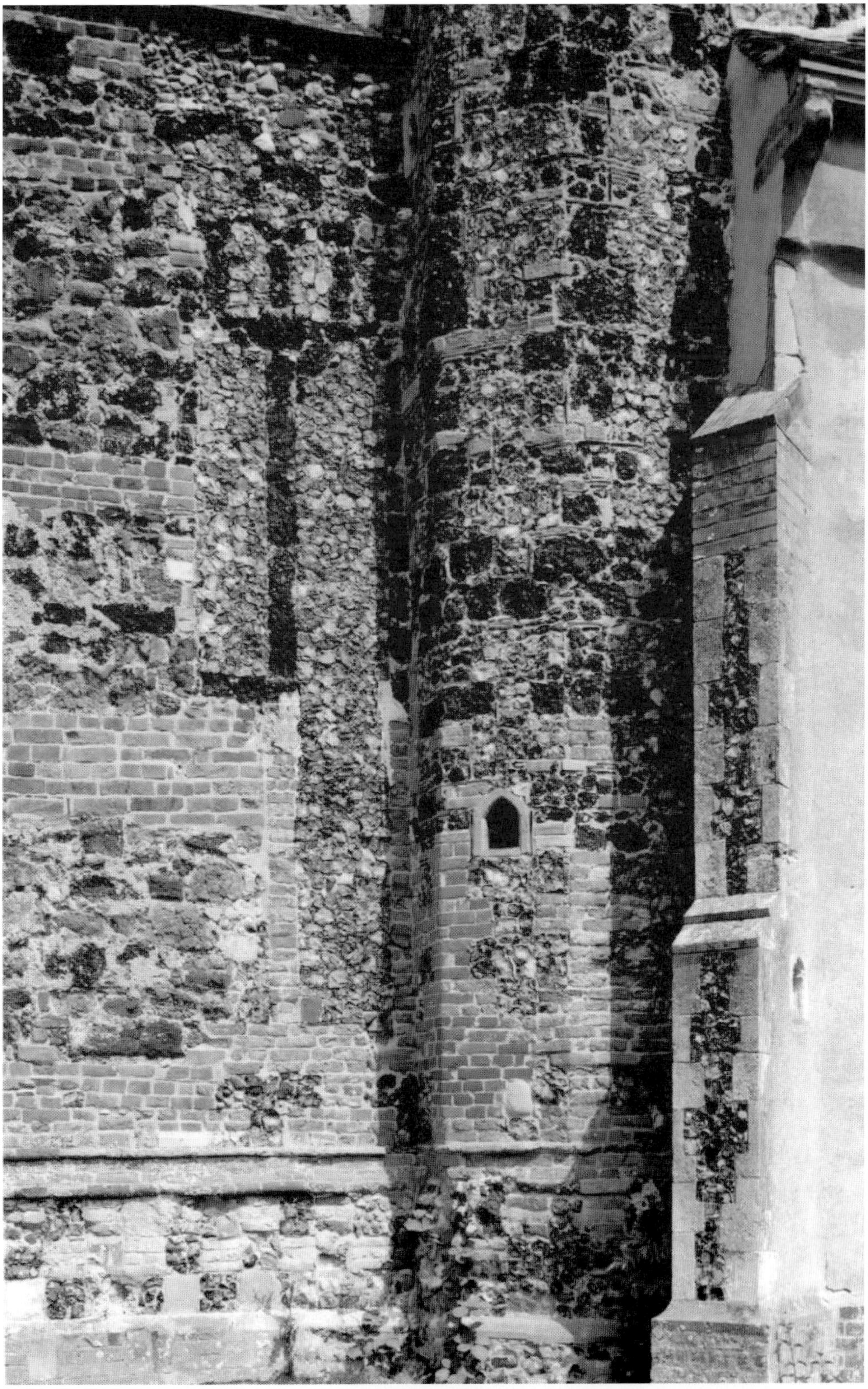

## PRITTLEWELL, mainly rubble stone.                   TQ 877868

| | |
|---|---|
| Tower: | 1B parapet with chequer. |
| South Porch: | Two-storey. Battlemented chequer parapet. |
| Parapets: | Battlemented with chequer on those of south aisle, chancel and nave north wall. |
| North Annex: | Single-storey modern with battlemented parapet having pairs of panels in each merlon. |

## RAWRETH                   TQ 781934

| | |
|---|---|
| North Porch: | Panelling on front and buttresses. Diagonal chequer on gable, the stone squares having shallow relief rosette decoration, and within each knapped flint square, a lozenge of red brickettes. |
| Clerestory: | Level parapet with two courses of chequer. |

## RIDGEWELL                   TL 740409

| | |
|---|---|
| Tower: | One course of chequer on base. Chequer on lower stages of buttresses. |

## ROCHFORD                   TQ 872903

| | |
|---|---|
| North Porch: | Stone. Chequer parapet but the stone squares are rough walling stone. |
| North Aisle: | Stone. Chequer parapet as porch. |

## ST OSYTH, Priory Gatehouse (50)                   TM 119156

| | |
|---|---|
| South Front:* | One of the most spectacular examples of flushwork. Above a base of repeated quatrefoils and a shallow panelled dado, the façade is horizontally bisected by a string course. Below this, the wall is panelled in three stages, a shallower band below two taller ones. Above the string course, there are two stages of panelling – short lower panels and upper ones almost three times higher, the latter paired below traceried canopy heads with crocketted finials and the mullion between each pair also being extended upwards as a crocketted finial. The deep battlemented parapet is chequered, partly with diagonal squares and partly with straight ones. |
| North Front: | Chequer band above the entrance arch; chequer on the parapets of the turrets flanking the archway and on the parapets between the turrets, diagonal in the centre bay and straight in the outer ones and on the turrets. |

## SALCOTT (VIII)                   TL 952137

| | |
|---|---|
| Tower: | 1S parapet with panelling. |

| | | |
|---|---|---|
| South Porch: | Panelled gable but the panel infillings are mixed flints and septaria in place of the normal knapped flint. | |

**SOUTHMINSTER**      TQ 958997

Tower:     Crag and cleft flint. Low-pitch gabled roof, north and south gables chequered.

**THORRINGTON**      TM 099198

Tower:     1S parapet with panelling.

# CAMBRIDGESHIRE

**BOTTISHAM (83)**      TL 545605

South Porch:     Built of clunch, but the wall below the side windows has two courses of an irregular chequer of limestone and knapped flint.

South Aisle:*     Built of stone. An early example of proudwork; squared knapped flint fills the spandrels between the arch

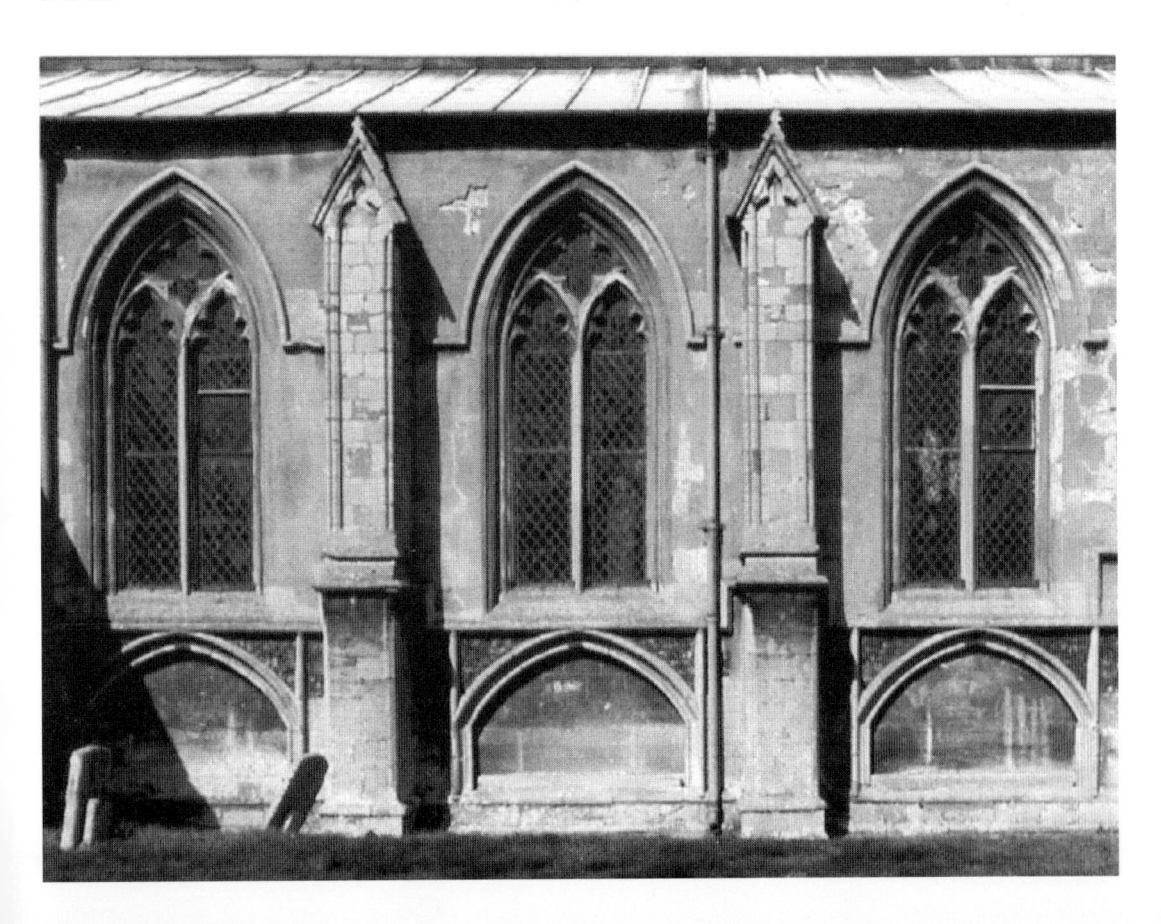

plate 83. Recessed knapped and squared flintwork in the spandrels above the blank arches below the windows of the south aisle of Bottisham church.

mouldings of the blank arcading dado and a horizontal string course below the aisle windows. Similar flintwork panels below the west windows of both aisles.

## BRINKLEY        TL 629548

Tower:        Chequer on base and on base of buttresses.

## DULLINGHAM        TL 632577

South Porch:        Chequer on base of front wall.
South Aisle:        Chequer on base.

## LITTLE WILBRAHAM        TL 546587

Tower:        1B parapet with short inverted T-shaped panels in merlons

## MARCH        TF 415952

Clerestory:*        Like the rest of the church, the clerestory is built of stone. A string course runs between the clerestory windows at the level of the bottom of the tracery; on the north side, above and below the string course, there are single flushwork emblems as at Bacton, and on the south side, emblems above the string course only, as at Cotton. The clerestory wall above the emblems on both sides is faced with knapped flint with alternating brick and flint voussoirs in the window arches.

## MELBOURN        TL 382448

Tower:        Chequer on base.
South Porch:        Two-storey. Panelling on base and chequer on parapets on front and side walls.

## PAMPISFORD        TL 498482

Tower:        On each diagonal buttress, one flushwork patée cross.

## PAPWORTH ST AGNES (VII)        TL 269645

All Walls:        Lapped chequer of ashlar stone blocks and 'squares' of mainly erratics and flint cobbles with some split flints. The stone blocks are slightly wider than square and the cobble areas generally a little narrower.

## SOHAM        TL 593732

Tower:        2S parapet with emblems and panelling in the upper

|  |  |
|---|---|
|  | stage and emblems in the frieze. Emblems on the base are interspersed with occasional panels and three little chequers vertically grouped. |
| North Porch: | Chequer on base and parapets of front and side walls. |

## STECHWORTH           TL 642590

Tower:     1B parapet with panelling.

## SWAFFHAM PRIOR, St Cyriac's        TL 568639

Tower:     Octagonal upper stage on square tower. 1B parapet with panelling.

# BEDFORDSHIRE

## LUTON, St Mary's           TL 096213

Walls:*     Walls of tower, north and south porches, aisles, north transept, and transept chapels: all in lapped chequer.

## TOTTENHOE           SP 988209

Chancel:     East wall lapped chequer. The stone squares are clunch.
Nave clerestory: Low-pitch battlemented parapet on east gable, with panels and emblems.

# BUCKINGHAMSHIRE

## PRINCES RISBOROUGH        SP 805035

Tower:     C.19. Level parapet below spire has four courses of chequer.

# HERTFORDSHIRE

## REDBOURN           TL 100116

Chancel:     Chequer on east wall and partially on south wall.
Church Hall:     Chequer on gables (modern).

# SURREY

### WOLDINGHAM            TQ 370560

Tower:      C.19. Halfway up the tower on the north, west and south walls, an inscription about 2 feet high in simulated Lombardic script reads:
Praise Him     and Magnify Him     For Ever.

# Appendix A

## BUILDINGS WITH PROUDWORK (churches except where otherwise stated)

| | |
|---|---|
| Aldburgh | On porch buttresses. |
| Banningham | On tower base and buttresses. |
| Barton Turf | Recessed flintwork in tower parapet. |
| Blakeney | On tower base and buttresses and north aisle buttresses. |
| Bottisham | Spandrels of blank arcading on south aisle. |
| Brisley | On tower buttresses. |
| Brome | Recessed flintwork on south porch and elsewhere. |
| Burnham Norton Friary | Feigned windows on east and west fronts. |
| Burnham Thorpe | Panels below east window. |
| Bylaugh | Feigned windows in belfry octagon. |
| Castle Acre | On tower parapet. |
| Chevington | On tower buttresses. |
| Cley-next-the-Sea | On north clerestory parapet and in frieze on south porch. |
| Cromer | On aisle buttresses. |
| Croxton | On chancel buttress. |
| Dalham | On upper stage of tower buttresses. |
| East Tuddenham | Feigned windows on porch front. |
| Fakenham | On tower buttresses. |
| Gipping | Feigned bay window on north annex. |
| Great Bromley | On south porch buttresses. |
| Great Massingham | On tower buttresses. |
| Hackford | On south porch buttresses. |
| Haveringland | On tower parapet, shallow. |
| Happisburgh | On tower base. |
| Hickling | On tower parapet, shallow. |
| Horham | On tower, below belfry openings. |

| | |
|---|---|
| Lowestoft | On aisle and chancel buttresses. |
| Mattishall | On tower parapet. |
| North Creake | On tower parapet. |
| North Elmham | On tower parapet and blank windows in tower. |
| North Tuddenham | On tower parapet. |
| Norwich, St Gregory's | On tower parapet. |
| Northwold | Blank windows in clerestory. |
| Poringland | Feigned windows in belfry octagon. |
| Quidenham | Feigned windows in belfry octagon. |
| Scarning | On south and west sides of tower base. |
| Shipdham | On tower parapet. |
| Shropham | On chancel buttresses. |
| Southrepps | On tower buttresses. |
| Southwold | On south porch. |
| Sporle | On tower parapet. |
| Stanford | Feigned windows in belfry octagon. |
| Swanton Morley | On base of west walls of tower and aisles. |
| Thorndon | On face of buttresses. |
| Thornham | On tower base and buttresses. |
| Thorpe St Andrew | On tower parapet. |
| Thwaite | On south aisle buttresses. |
| Weasenham All Saints | On base of south porch. |
| Weasenham St Peter | On base of nave. |
| Wells-next-the-Sea | On tower parapet. |
| Wickham Market | Feigned windows in belfry octagon. |
| Wickmere | On south porch. |
| Wiggenhall St Germans | On tower parapet. |
| Winterton | On tower parapet. |
| Woodbridge | On base of north aisle. |
| Wymondham | On two eastern bays of north clerestory and upper stages of west tower buttresses. |

# Appendix B

## CHURCHES WITH BRICK FLUSHWORK

| | |
|---|---|
| Ardleigh | Tower parapet. |
| Ashwellthorpe | Tower parapet. |
| Bergh Apton | Tower parapet. |
| Bredfield | Tower parapet. |
| Burgh St Peter | Tower base. |
| Caistor St Edmund | Tower parapet. |
| Feering | Porch base. |
| Great Ashfield | Porch. |
| Great Barton | Porch base. |
| Great Bealings | Porch base. |
| Great Witchingham | Clerestory. |
| Great Yarmouth, St Spiridon | Tower parapet. |
| Gosbeck | North vestry. |
| Hardwick | Porch. |
| Ixworth Thorpe | Porch parapet. |
| Lawford | Chancel. |
| Little Massingham | Tower stair turret. |
| New Buckenham | Tower parapet. |
| North Cove | Porch gable. |
| Norwich, St Benedict's | Feigned belfry windows. |
| Old Catton | Tower octagon. |
| Ringsfield | Tower parapet. |
| Roughton | Tower parapet. |
| Saxlingham | Tower parapet. |
| West Winch | Gable peak of porch. |
| Weybourne | Porch. |
| Weybread | Feigned belfry windows. |

# Appendix C

## SHALLOW-SUNK STONE HEADS TO FLUSHWORK PANELS

| | |
|---|---|
| Bardwell | Porch. |
| Breckles | Porch. |
| Broome | Tower parapet. |
| East Dereham | Porch. |
| Ellingham | Tower parapet. |
| Filby | Tower parapet. |
| Finningham | Porch. |
| Foxley | Tower parapet. |
| Mattishall | Porch. |
| Postwick | Bases of tower buttresses. |
| Pulham St Mary | Porch. |
| Thornham Magna | Porch. |
| Weybourne | Tower parapet. |
| Whissonsett | Tower Parapet. |
| Wickhampton | Tower Parapet. |

# Appendix D

## 'NORWICH' STYLE FLUSHWORK ON CHURCH TOWER PARAPETS

Blofield

Burgh next Aylsham

Burgh St Margaret (Fleggburgh)

Burlingham St Andrew

Coltishall

Ditchingham

Erpingham

Griston

Northrepps

Norwich, St Clement's

Norwich, St George's, Colegate

Norwich, St George's, Tombland

Norwich, St John-le-Sepulchre

Westwick

# Bibliography

Baggallay, F.T., *The Use of Flint in Buildings especially in the County of Suffolk*.
R.I.B.A. Transactions, New Series, Vol. I, pp.105-24. 1885

Blatchly, J. and Northeast, P., *Decoding Flint Flushwork on Suffolk and Norfolk Churches*,
Suffolk Institute of Archaeology and History, 2005

Clifton Taylor, A., *The Pattern of English Building*, Faber, 4th edn, 1987

Clifton Taylor, A., and Ireson, A.S., *English Stone Building*, Gollancz, 1983

Hart, S., *Flint Architecture of East Anglia*, Giles de la Mare, 2000

Pevsner, N. and Others, *The Buildings of England*, Penguin:

    *Cambridgeshire* 1970

    *Essex* 1965

    *Norfolk 1: Norwich & North-East* 1997

    *Norfolk 2: North-West & South* 1999

    *Suffolk* 1974

Talbot, M., *Medieval Flushwork of East Anglia*, Poppyland Publishing, 2004